VIENNA 1900
Architecture and Painting

The following volumes in this series are in preparation:
VIENNA 1900 – Music
VIENNA 1900 – Literature
MUNICH 1900 – Architecture and Painting

Published in March 1984

Layout and jacket design (using Josef Diveky's "Wiener Werk-stätte" postcard No 405, 'The Church at Steinhof') by Christian Brandstätter and Christian M. Nebehay.
Readers Günter Treffer and Christine Wessely, technical editor Franz Hanns.
Printed and bound by Wiener Verlag, Himberg. Illustrations by Reproform, Vienna. Set in Palatino-Antiqua by RSB, Vienna.

Copyright © 1983 by Christian Brandstätter Verlag & Edition, Vienna
ISBN 3-85447-027-4

Christian Brandstätter Verlag & Edition Gesellschaft m.b.H. & Co KG
A-1080 Wien, Wickenburggasse 26, Tel. (0222) 48 38 14-15

Christian M. Nebehay

VIENNA
❧ 1900 ❧

Architecture and Painting

❧ Where to find ❧

WAGNER	OLBRICH
KLIMT	SCHIELE
MOSER	LOOS
HOFFMANN	KOKOSCHKA

Lives and Works · Memorial Sites
Museums and Collections in Vienna

With 310 illustrations, 72 in colour, and 62 maps designed by the
author and drawn by Irmgard Grillmayer

Translated from the German by
Renée Nebehay-King

Verlag Christian Brandstätter · Wien

LEGEND

1   Postsparkasse—*Post Office Savings Bank* (O. Wagner)
2   Kunstgewerbeschule, jetzt: Hochschule für
    angewandte Kunst (*Arts and Crafts College*, now
    Academy of Applied Arts)
3   Minerva-Brunnen—*Minerva Fountain* (F. Laufberger)
4   Mus. f. angew. Kunst—*Museum of Applied Arts*
5   [Zedlitzhalle (Kokoschka, Schiele)]
6   [Gartenbaugesellschaft—*Horticultural
    Society* (Secession)]
7   U-Bahn-Station—*Underground station* Stadtpark
    (O. Wagner)
8   Konzerthaus [Kunstschau—*Art-Show*]
9   Jugoslawische Botschaft—*Yugoslav Embassy*
    (O. Wagner)
10 Österr. Galerie, 19. and 20. Jahrhundert—
    Gallery of Austrian Art (Belvedere)
11 Museum des 20. Jhdt.—*Museum of 20th Century Art*
12 Zentralfriedhof—*Central Cemetery* (P. Altenberg,
    A. Loos)
13 [Salon Pisko (Egon Schiele)]
14 [Galerie Arnot (Egon Schiele)]
15 Hist. Museum der Stadt Wien—*City of Vienna,
    Historical Museum*
16 [A. Loos' Wohnung—*apartment*]
17 Stadtbahnstationen—*City Railway stations*
    (O. Wagner)
18 Café Museum (A. Loos)
19 Akademie der bildenden Künste—
    Academy of Fine Arts
20 O.-Wagner-Denkmal—*Memorial* (J. Hoffmann)
21 Secession
22 [Casa Piccola, Salon Flöge]
23 Kunsthist. Mus.—*Museum of the History of Arts*
24 Albertina
25 Theater-Museum—*Theatre Museum*
26 Österr. Nationalbibliothek—*Austrian National Library*
27 Theseus-Tempel / project (J. Hoffmann)
28 Burgtheater
29 Stadiongasse No 10 (O. Wagner)
30 Stadtbibliothek, Rathaus—*Library, Town Hall*
31 Universität—*University*
32 Universitätsstrasse No 12 (O. Wagner)
33 N.Ö.Landes-Mus.—*Lower Austrian County Museum*
34 Loos-Haus—*Loos house*
35 Buchhandlung—*Bookshop* Manz (A. Loos)
36 Parfümerie—*Cosmetics shop* Ruttner (A. Loos)
37 Schneider—*Outfitter* Leschka (A. Loos)
38 Schneider—*Outfitter* Kniže (A. Loos)
39 'Anker-Haus'—*Anker house* (O. Wagner)
40 Bonbons—*Sweetshop* Altmann (J. Hoffmann)
41 Ankeruhr—*'Anker' clock* (F. Matsch)
42 Schützenhaus—*Lockhouse* (O. Wagner)
43 'American Bar' (A. Loos)
44 Lobmeyr-Gläser—*glasses* (J. Hoffmann, A. Loos)
45 [Fledermaus cabaret]
46 Palais Esterházy [Wiener Werkstätte]
47 Mus. mod. Kunst—*Museum of Modern Art*
    (Palais Liechtenstein)

[] = no longer extant

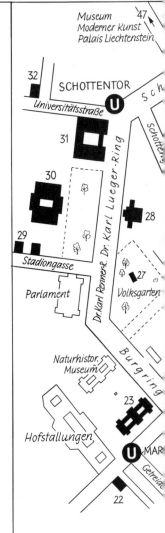

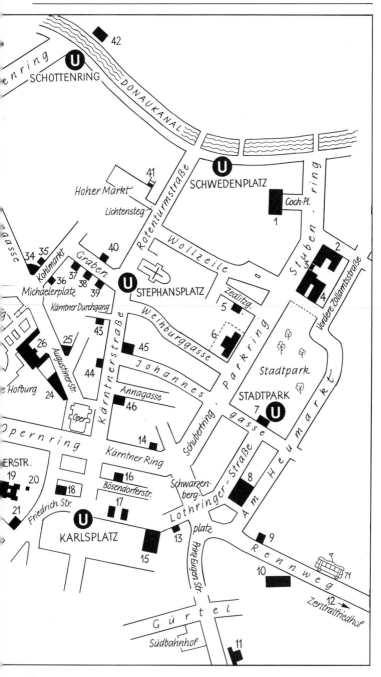

ACKNOWLEDGMENTS

The publishers and the author are grateful to Ing. Norbert Gradisch, Vienna, for permission to reproduce the works of Egon Schiele; to the Verlag Welz, Salzburg, for Gustav Klimt; and to Cosmopress, Geneva, for Oskar Kokoschka. Thanks are also due to all museums, collections, libraries and archives in Vienna, Graz, Linz etc. and to all private individuals whose co-operation has helped to publish this book.

Academy of Fine Arts, Vienna, p. VII/23; Albertina, Vienna, p. II/5, II/11 (above r.), II/13 (below), II/17, II/22 (above); Egon Schiele Archives, Albertina, Vienna, p. II/4 below, II/6 above, II/11 below, II/13 above, II/14 below, II/19 above; Adolf Loos Archives, Albertina, Vienna, p. VIII/4, VIII/5, VIII/8, VIII/9, VIII/18 above r., VIII/19, VIII/21; Herbert Asenbaum, Vienna, p. V/9 below r.; Picture Archives of the Austrian National Library, Vienna, p. I/8 above, III/17 below, III/19 below, V/9 above, V/10; Picture Archives Christian Brandstätter Verlag & Edition, Vienna, p. I/7 above, I/16, I/18 above, I/19 above, I/20, I/22 above, II/1, II/16 above, III/7 below, III/8, III/9, III/10, III/12, III/16 above, III/23, IV/1, IV/3, IV/4, IV/5, IV/6, IV/7, IV/11, IV/13, IV/15, IV/16, IV/17, IV/18, IV/19, IV/20, IV/21, IV/22, IV/23, V/1, V/3, V/4 above, V/5, V/6, V/7, V/8, V/11, VI/1, VI/2 above, VI/4 below, VI/6, VI/10, VII/6 above, VII/7, VII/8, VII/9, VII/13, VII/14, VII/15, VII/24, VIII/1, VIII/6 below, VIII/7, VIII/10, VIII/11 below, VIII/13, VIII/14 above l., VIII/18 above l., VIII/23 above r.; Collection Christian Brandstätter, Vienna, p. I/1, I/7 below, I/9, II/15 below, III/7 above, IV/8 above, VI/5, VI/7, VII/3 above, VII/11 below, VIII/12; Walter und Marianne Feilchenfeldt, Zürich, p. III/17 above, III/18 below; Photo Johanna Fiegl, Vienna, p. VII/5, VII/6 below, VII/16, VII/17, VII/18, VII/19, VIII/18 below, VIII/20; Photo Gerlach, Vienna, p. VIII/22 above, VIII/14 below, VIII/16, VIII/22 above; City of Vienna Historical Museum, p. II/7 below, II/9 below, II/12 centre, II/12 below, II/16 below, II/20 above, III/11 above l.; Photo Franz Hubmann, Vienna, p. VIII/14 above r.; Julius Hummel, Vienna, p. III/11 above r.; Kniže, Vienna, p. VIII/15; Oskar Kokoschka Documentation Centre, Pöchlarn, p.III/1, III/4, III/5, III/6, III/13, III/16 below, III/22; Art Museum, Basle (photo Erich Lessing), p. III/19 above; J. & L. Lobmeyr, Vienna, p. VIII/22 below; National Gallery, Berlin, p. III/15; Archives Professor Christian M. Nebehay, Vienna, p. I/2, I/3, I/4, I/5, I/6, I/8 below, I/10 above, I/11 r., I/12, I/13, I/14, I/17, I/21, I/22 below, I/23, II/3, II/8 above, II/9 above, II/12 above, II/15 above, II/18 above, II/23 below, III/11 below, III/21, IV/10, IV/14, VI/2 below, VI/3, VI/4 above, VI/9, VI/11, VI/12, VII/1, VII/2, VII/3 below, VII/4; Neue Galerie, Graz (Foto Fürböck, Graz), p. II/6 below, II/11 above l.; Neue Galerie der Stadt Linz, p. II/10 below, III/14 below; Niederösterreichisches Landesmuseum, Vienna, p. II/19 below; Österreichische Galerie, Vienna (Foto Otto, Vienna), p. II/7 centre, II/18 below, II/21 below, II/22 below; Österreichisches Museum für angewandte Kunst, Vienna, p. V/9 below l., VI/8, VII/10, VII/12, VII/21 above; Burkhard Rukschcio, Vienna, p. VIII/4 above, VIII/8 above l. and below r.; Archives Werner J. Schweiger, Vienna (Foto Wolfgang Lampert, Vienna), p. II/7 above, II/8 below, II/14 above, II/23 above, III/3, III/24, VII/11 above; Verlag–Galerie Welz, Salzburg, p. I/10 below, I/11 l., I/15, I/18 below, I/19, III/14 above, III/18 above, III/20; Photo Ingo Wessely, Vienna, p. IV/8 below, IV/12, V/4 below, VII/20, VII/21 below, VII/22 below, VIII/6 above, VIII/11 above, VIII/17, VIII/23 above l., VIII/23 below; Wiener Stadt- und Landesbibliothek p. II/10 above.

Vienna · Inner City Map
4/5

Acknowledgements
6

Preface
8

GUSTAV KLIMT
I/1−I/24

EGON SCHIELE
II/1−II/24

OSKAR KOKOSCHKA
III/1−III/24

OTTO WAGNER
IV/1−IV/24

JOSEPH MARIA OLBRICH
V/1−V/12

KOLO MOSER
VI/1−VI/12

JOSEF HOFFMANN
VII/1−VII/24

ADOLF LOOS
VIII/1−VIII/24

VIENNA 1900 — ARCHITECTURE AND PAINTING is a new-style guide designed to help the reader find buildings and works of art dating from the turn of the century and to draw his attention to much that might otherwise—unjustifiably—escape notice. The scale of values is tipping: what we disdained and rejected only a short while ago is now the object of our admiration. (This goes not only for Vienna but also, to take an instance, for Scotland where, after a similar delay, Mackintosh is coming into his own again.) There is no doubt that at the time itself—around 1900—Vienna was a magnet that attracted well-known artists from all over Europe, who exhibited their work in the "Secession" and in so doing provided fruitful stimuli for the native artists. The result was an unmistakable Viennese style and the "Vienna Art Spring", which lasted from 1898 to 1905 and was, as we now see, considerably more important than had been assumed.

This guide shows a selection of the most important—and above all accessible—works of art. It lays no claim to completeness; but the reader's attention is drawn to the list of recommended literature provided at the end of each chapter. There are eight self-contained sections, each section being devoted to one artist. Detailed maps show the reader how to get—mostly by public transport (underground)—to the buildings and works of art mentioned in the text. It is relatively easy, by strolling through the inner city, to discover what is left of architect Adolf Loos's creations; but in the case of Otto Wagner, for instance, it takes more time—and a spirit of enterprise—to find his buildings along the Danube Canal, his "Stadtbahn" (City Railway) stations, or even his remarkable villas in Hütteldorf. Again, it is doubtful whether any Viennese—let alone a visitor to the city—has ever been to see Olbrich's modest but characteristic building in the Rustenschacher Allee, built in 1898 as a clubhouse for the Civil Servants' Cycling Club and now housing a tennis club. And who, looking up at Ferstel's splendid ceiling in the Great Hall of Vienna University, with its centre panel by F. Matsch, stops to think that this was to be the setting for Klimt's famous "faculty paintings", which perished in the flames in 1945?

The Viennese museums nearly all close at 16 hours. This leaves the visitor ample time to go on the numerous excursions to which this guide invites him. It is hoped to keep the Kunsthistorisches Museum open until 18 hours from Tuesday to Friday as from early summer 1984.   *Ch. M. Nebehay*

GUSTAV KLIMT
1862–1918

GUSTAV KLIMT · 1862–1918

Gustav Klimt was born in Vienna on July 16th 1862. His father Ernst Klimt (1834–1892) was an engraver and had a hard time earning enough to feed his large family on. At the age of fourteen Gustav won a scholarship which enabled him to attend the Arts & Crafts College from 1876 to 1883. His two brothers also became artists: Ernst (1864–1892) took up painting and Georg (1861–1931) metal work.

It was years before Klimt shook off his teachers' influence. In 1883 he and his brother Ernst joined up with Franz Matsch (1861–1942): together they formed an "artists' trio", set up a studio and began doing decorative work for theatres outside Vienna. They got two state commissions in 1886–88 and 1891: decorations for the staircases in the new Burgtheater and for the Museum of the History of Art. Gustav Klimt twice earned special praise from Emperor Franz Joseph I., but was not subsequently employed by the court.

It took him a long time to recover from the crisis following the deaths of his brother and his father (1892). When the young artists flocked to him and in 1897 founded the Secession, of which he was the first president, he had as yet produced no painting in what was later to be his definitive style; but now came the breakthrough with his portrait of Sonja Knips, and from that moment onwards he was, for the rest of his life, at the hub of the modern art movement. Much of what happened in the Secession in those wonderful years of the "Vienna Spring" between 1898 and 1905 owes its impetus to his generous and selfless nature. His friendship towards artists, and in particular towards the young and rising talents (e. g. Oskar Kokoschka, Egon Schiele) was exemplary.

He made his name as a portraitist of beautiful society women. But his best work is probably to

be found in his drawings, of which some 4000 are still extant: they are mostly sketches for his portraits (there are sometimes as many as 150 for one portrait, each one showing a different detail, with the actual features of the sitter being only hinted at in a few "shorthand" strokes). He was a very slow painter: some of his landscapes took him several months, during which he spent hours on even the smallest detail. As a distraction from this strenuous work he always had professional models standing about in his studio, whom—fascinated as he was by the beauty of the female body—he would draw. Many of his drawings are mildly erotic, never offensive. Visitors reported that the sketches lay piled up on the floor of his studio; occasionally he would exhibit some of them, and this established his reputation as one of the best draughtsmen of his time; but he never sold them, and this explains why they are mostly unsigned and undated.

Klimt remained unmarried. There were women, however, who shared his life for a while and bore him children. His longest attachment was to Emilie Flöge, the sister of his sister-in-law; he stayed with her until his death. He never taught, his application for a professorship at the Academy having been repeatedly refused, probably on account of the—by modern standards incomprehensible—scandals occasioned by his larger paintings. He died on February 6th 1918. For a long time he was forgotten. Only since the sixties has he come into his own again.

Left page: Vignette from 'Ver Sacrum'. Both pages: Symbols drawn by Klimt for the plates of 'The Works of Gustav Klimt', 1908—14 (Albertina).

Klimt's birthplace in the 13th district (XIII.), 247 Linzer Strasse (destroyed 1967).

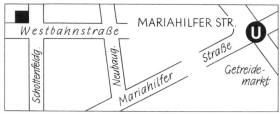

Until his death Klimt lived in the flat of his mother, Anna, née Finster (1836−1915) at VII., 36/III Westbahnstrasse.

Klimt's teachers at the Kunstgewerbeschule (Arts & Crafts College) I., 5 Stubenring, were Ferdinand Laufberger (1828−1881), who among other things designed the mosaics for the Minerva Well; and Julius v. Berger (1850−1902).

1 *Former Gartenbaugesellschaft*
2 *Museum of Applied Arts*
3 *Minerva Well*
4 *Arts & Crafts College (now Academy of Applied Arts)*

Gustav Klimt had a studio at VI., 8 Sandwirtgasse, together with his brother Ernst and Franz Matsch. The angel on the ceiling of the staircase was painted by one of the three artists.

Ernst Klimt painted a portrait of his wife Helene (née Flöge) in the "German Renaissance" lunette above the main staircase of the Museum of the History of Art. To her right is a portrait of her Father Ernst Flöge. Klimt's own father was the model for the "Netherlands" lunette.

Franz Matsch, the third of the artists' trio, designed among other things the decorative clock ("Ankeruhr") at I., 10/11 Hoher Markt.

Gustav Klimt, "Interior of the Old Burgtheater", 1888, water colour (Hist. Museum).

DECORATIONS IN THE BURGTHEATER · 1886–1888

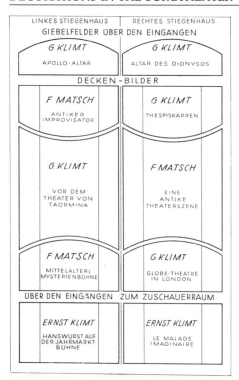

LINKES STIEGENHAUS	RECHTES STIEGENHAUS
GIEBELFELDER ÜBER DEN EINGÄNGEN	
G KLIMT APOLLO·ALTAR	**G KLIMT** ALTAR DES DIONYSOS
DECKEN-BILDER	
F MATSCH ANTIKER IMPROVISATOR	**G KLIMT** THESPISKARREN
G. KLIMT VOR DEM THEATER VON TAORMINA	**F MATSCH** EINE ANTIKE THEATERSZENE
F MATSCH MITTELALTERL. MYSTERIENBÜHNE	**G KLIMT** GLOBE-THEATRE IN LONDON
ÜBER DEN EINGÄNGEN ZUM ZUSCHAUERRAUM	
ERNST KLIMT HANSWURST AUF DER JAHRMARKT-BÜHNE	**ERNST KLIMT** LE MALADE IMAGINAIRE

Plan showing the work of the three young artists in the staircases of the Burgtheater.

Gustav Klimt, "The Globe Theatre in London" (detail). On the left, the only existing self-portrait in oils (wearing ruff); leaning against column, Ernst; between them, Franz Matsch.

Left staircase. Centre panel: Klimt's "The Theatre in Taormina". The Burgtheater, opened in 1888 and built by Carl von Hasenauer (1833–1894) after his and Gottfried Semper's (1803–1879) plans (Inner City Map No 28).

The Museum of the History of Art, I., 5 Burgring (Inner City Map No 23), was built in 1872−1881 by Carl v. Hasenauer. The decoration of the main staircase was the only official commission ever given to Hans Makart. He made sketches, but owing to his untimely death was not able to complete more than the lunettes. Michael v. Munkáczy (1844−1909)−then a celebrated artist−was entrusted with the ceiling paintings; and the decoration of the intercolumnar and spandrel spaces fell to the "Artists' Trio", who were required to keep to the programme outlined by Albert Ilg (1847−1896), director of the arts and crafts collections.

Gustav Klimt executed the following: Florentine Quattrocento and Cinquecento−Roman and Venetian Quattrocento−Antique Greece (left: here Klimt shook off his academic style for the first time and, unnoticed, painted Glykene, Pausanias' beloved, as a modern girl of his day). −Egypt−Primitive Italian Art.

Top of page: Museum of the History of Art main staircase: The lunettes show portraits of famous artists and are by Hans Makart (1840−1884). Shown here: "Leonardo da Vinci".

For the first exhibition of the Secession in the building of the "Gartenbaugesellschaft" (built 1859–1863 by August Weber, no longer extant (Inner City Map No 6). Gustav Klimt designed the poster (now in the Albertina). The censor took objection to Theseus' nakedness and insisted on a tree being overprinted.

The Secession was founded in 1897 following the exodus of young artists from the "Künstlerhaus", Austria's leading artist association, where they felt neglected. They rallied around Gustav Klimt, who became their first President and set the tone until the Klimt group in its turn left the Secession. The first exhibition was a great success. 218 items were sold and there were more than 57.000 visitors. Venerable Rudolf von Alt (1812–1905), a distinguished water-colourist, had joined the Secession and asked Emperor Francis Joseph I. to honour them with his presence. The Emperor, a patron of the arts if not their champion, visited the Secession once only, and Gustav Klimt, as President, was there to receive him.

The "Gartenbaugesellschaft" building (later pulled down); in the background the Palais Coburg, in the foreground the newly planted trees of the Ringstrasse. About 1870.

Both paintings: "Love" (Hist. Museum) and "Actor Josef Lewinsky as Carlos in Clavigo" (Österr. Galerie) were done in 1895 and are typical examples of the slightly sugary style Klimt was trying to overcome.

At the time the Secession was founded, Klimt had not yet had his breakthrough as an artist. It came in 1898, when he painted the portrait of Sonja Knips.

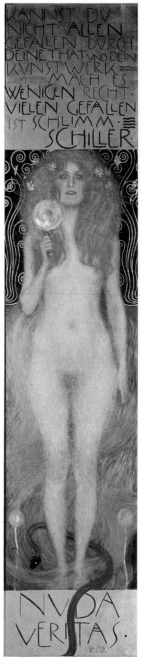

From 1892 to 1914 Klimt had a studio in the back garden of VIII., 21 Josefstädter Strasse. (A modern building has replaced the original one; the house entrance leads to a courtyard and a strip of grass. On the far side of the grass is a high boundary wall, in front of which Klimt's studio once stood.)

The furnishings were by Josef Hoffmann and are still partly extant. A painting by Klimt can be seen on the wall: "Die Hoffnung", 1907/8 (private collection, Vienna).

Left: "Nuda veritas", 1899. Originally the property of the author and critic Hermann Bahr (1863−1934), one of the great champions of the Modern Style (Österr. Nationalbibliothek, Theatre Collection).

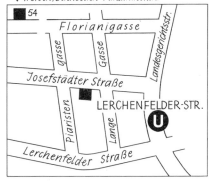

I/11

"Hygieia", detail from "Medicine". This colour reproduction made in 1931 gives an idea of the colouring of the paintings, which were destroyed during the war.

30. X. 1892	A bank credit is granted for the decoration of the Great Hall of the Vienna University.
4. IX. 1893	Franz Matsch's proposal is refused.
4. IX. 1894	Klimt is commissioned to paint the three pictures "Philosophy", "Jurisprudence" and "Medicine" and 10 spandrel pictures. Matsch is to paint "Theology" and the centrepiece "Triumph of Light over Darkness", the total fee amounting to 60.000 Gulden.
III. 1900	Scandal caused by the exhibition of "Philosophy". Protest by the university professors.
1904	Klimt turns down the commission for the 10 spandrel paintings.
3. IV. 1905	Klimt withdraws his three ceiling paintings.
25. V. 1905	August Lederer, art patron, buys the "Philosophy". Klimt reimburses his fee.
1911	Kolo Moser buys "Medicine" and "Jurisprudence".
11. V. 1945	The three paintings are destroyed by fire at Schloss Immendorf in Lower Austria, where they had been sent for safekeeping during World War II.

From A. Strobl: The University Paintings of G. Klimt, Albertina Studies II (1964). It was Dr. Strobl who conceived the idea of photo-copying the four paintings into the present empty spaces.

Above left: Franz Matsch, "Theology" (Dean's room of the Faculty of Theology, Vienna University).

Above right: Gustav Klimt, "Jurisprudence", 1903–1907 (destroyed by fire in 1945).

Centre: Franz Matsch, "Triumph of Light over Darkness" (ceiling painting. Great Hall, Vienna University).

Below left and right: Gustav Klimt, "Medicine" (1900–1907) and "Philosophy" (1899–1907), destroyed by fire in 1945.

The splitting of the commission between two artists whose styles had grown apart was not a happy idea. It must be said that Matsch's "Theology" would have looked better in the somewhat overdecorated ceiling than Klimt's smaller-scale paintings. Klimt had originally also thought on larger lines, but with time he had gradually come away from the sketches he had submitted, this probably being one of the main reasons for the university professors' protest.

Max Klinger (1857–1920), "Beethoven". Completed on 25th March 1902, displayed at the 14th exhibition of the Secession on 15th April (Inner City Map No 21). The city of Leipzig bought the sculpture (for 250.000 Marks) before Vienna could make an offer. It now stands in the entrance of the new "Gewandhaus" in Leipzig.

The Secession artists, convinced that this was the greatest sculpture of its time, gave it a welcome which must surely be unique in the history of modern art. They all—without payment—helped decorate the rooms. Klimt's Beethoven Frieze, which is nearly 90 feet long, is one of the most important works of art of the Art Nouveau period, and is at present being restored.

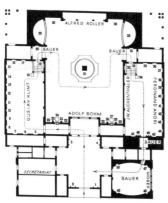

Plan of the exhibition (from the catalogue of the 14th Secession exhibition, Albertina).
Above: Klimt's Beethoven Frieze in the exhibition room (left); in the central room (right) Klinger's Beethoven sculpture.

Above: "The Longing for Happiness Finds Appeasement in Poetry". (Detail from the righthand section of the frieze).

Below: "The Supplications of the Weak to the Armoured Strong". (Detail from the lefthand section of the frieze.)

Gustav Klimt: Portrait of Emilie Flöge (1902) (Hist. Museum).

The three sisters, Emilie, Helene and Paula Flöge, ran one of Vienna's leading fashion salons in the "Casa piccola", VI., Ib, Mariahilfer Strasse. Helene married Ernst Klimt. Gustav spent almost every summer between 1900 and 1918 with Emilie on the Attersee.

Above left: Emilie Flöge in the garden of her house on the Attersee. Photograph by Gustav Klimt. About 1905.

Above right: Emilie Flöge. Photograph by d'Ora-Benda, Vienna, 1909.

The portrait (left), painted in 1902, was not to the liking of either Emilie or Klimt. Shortly after its completion it was sold to the Historical Museum of Vienna.

Right: Reception room in the Flöge salon. Interior decoration by Kolo Moser (1868–1918). (No longer extant).

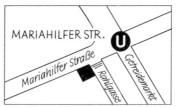

Klimt created a mosaic frieze for the dining-room of the Palais Stoclet in Brussels (above), built 1905—1909 and one of Josef Hoffmann's masterpieces, the interior of which has remained unchanged to this day. The cartoons for the frieze (Museum of Applied Arts, Inner City Map No 4) were restored some years ago. "Expectation" (below left), "Fulfilment" (below right).

When they left the Secession in 1905 the Klimt group lost their exhibition rooms. On the site of what was to be the Konzerthaus (Inner City Map No 8), Josef Hoffmann put up makeshift pavilions for the "Kunstschau". The first exhibition showed Austrian, the second international modern art. Oskar Kokoschka (1908, 1909) and Egon Schiele (1909) were among the exhibitors.

"The Kiss", Klimt's major work, 1907/8, was acquired by the Österreichische Galerie in 1909.

Gustav Klimt: "Park Alley at Schloss Kammer", 1912 (Österr. Galerie).

There are no landscape sketches by Klimt. It is known that he carried with him on his walks a small ivory shield with a rectangular opening cut into it, through which he looked.

Klimt started painting landscapes relatively late in his career. Most of his landscapes were begun on the Attersee and were completed in his studio, often after months of work. It is still possible to trace his subjects on the spot (see plan).

1 "Island in the Attersee", about 1901 (private collection, New York). 2 "Schloss Kammer on the Attersee I–IV", 1908–1912: I (Národný Galerie, Prague), II (private collection, USA), III (Österreichische Galerie), IV (private collection, Vienna). – "Park Alley at Schloss Kammer", 1912 (Österreichische Galerie). 3 "Litzlbergkeller", 1915/16 (private collection, Vienna). – 4 "Forester's house in Weissenbach", 1914/16 (private collection, USA). – 5 "House in Unterach", 1916 (W. Gurlitt Museum, Linz). – "Church in Unterach", about 1916 (private collection, Graz).

Klimt saw to it that his works reached a wider public during his lifetime by means of reproductions. "Das Werk Gustav Klimts" (The Works of Gustav Klimt) appeared from 1908 to 1914 in 50 reproductions, printed under the supervision of the artist. Ten of them (Albertina!) were in colour, with gold and no less than 16 colours superimposed! It is worth recording that Emperor Francis Joseph I subscribed to the first copy. "Gustav Klimt, 25 Handzeichnungen, zum Teil farbige Lichtdrucke, Wien 1919" (Gustav Klimt, 25 reproductions of drawings, some in colour, Vienna 1919) (Albertina), appeared immediately after Klimt's death. The illustration shows No 16, drawn in 1916. Klimt's drawings are at present being catalogued (see Bibliography).

Klimt's last studio was in XIII., 11 Feldmühlgasse. Egon Schiele's efforts to preserve it were unsuccessful: the house was converted into apartments. On the easels, "The Bride", 1917/18 (Österreichische Galerie, on loan) and "Lady with Fan", 1917/18 (private collection, Vienna), both uncompleted.

Klimt's smock (Modeschule, Fashion School, Schloss Hetzendorf).

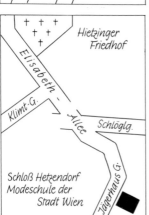

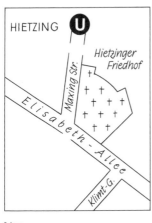

Klimt suffered a stroke in his home on 11th January 1918. He died in the Allgemeines Krankenhaus on 6th February 1918, a victim of the influenza epidemic that raged in the city, taking a death toll higher than the casualties in World War I. His grave is in the Hietzing cemetery, Group 5, No 194/5. The plan to have a sarcophagus designed by Josef Hoffmann was not carried out. To this day, admirers of Klimt lay flowers on his grave.

WHERE TO FIND:

PAINTINGS:
Österr. Galerie = Österreichische Galerie des 19. & 20. Jahrhunderts (Gallery of Austrian Art, 19th & 20th cent.), III., Oberes Belvedere (Inner City Map No 10). Open: Tues., Wed., Thurs., Sat. 10−16 hours, Fri. 10−13 hours, Sun. 9−12 hours. Closed on Mondays.

Mus. mod. Kunst = Museum moderner Kunst (Museum of Modern Art), Palais Liechtenstein, IX., 1 Fürstengasse (Inner City Map No 47). Open: Mon., Wed., Thurs., Fri., Sat., Sun. 10−18 hours. Closed on Tuesdays.

Österreichisches Theatermuseum (Austrian Theatre Museum), I., 3 Hanusch-gasse (next to the Albertina). Memorial room Anna Bahr-Mildenburg. Open: Tues., Thurs. 11 hours. Apply to the Kasse der Bundestheater (National Theatre Box Office) at I., 3 Hanuschgasse. Later the museum will be at Palais Lobkowitz, I., 2 Lobkowitzplatz (Inner City Map No 25).

PAINTINGS AND DRAWINGS:
Hist. Mus. = Historisches Museum der Stadt Wien (City of Vienna Historical Museum), IV., Karlsplatz (Inner City Map No 15). Open: Tues., Wed., Thurs. 10−19 hours, Fri. 10−16 hours, Sat. 14−18 hours, Sun. 9−17 hours. Closed on Mondays.

DRAWINGS:
Albertina = Graphische Sammlung Albertina, I., 1 Augustinerstrasse (Inner City Map No 24), printroom (also housing the Klimt Archives). Open: Mon., Tues., Wed., Thurs. 13−16 hours. Closed Fri., Sat., Sun.

DECORATIVE WORK:
Kunsthist. Mus. = Kunsthistorisches Museum (Museum of the History of Art), I., 5 Burgring (Inner City Map No 23), staircase. Open: Tues., Wed., Thurs., Fri. 10−16 hours, Sat., Sun. 9−16 hours, Tues., Fri. 19−21 hours. Closed Mondays.

Burgtheater, I., Dr.-Karl-Lueger-Ring (Inner City Map No 28), staircases. To visit, telephone Gebäudeverwaltung (administrative office) 52 24 0, or enter just before the evening performance (with ticket).

University, I., 1 Dr.-Karl-Lueger-Ring (Inner City Map No 31), Great Hall: ceiling painting by Franz Matsch, weekdays 8−16 hours; theological faculty: "Theology" by Franz Matsch (by appointment, tel. 43 00 0).

Mus. f. angew. Kunst = Österreichisches Museum für angewandte Kunst (Museum of Applied Art), I., 5 Stubenring (Inner City Map No 4). Sketches for the Stoclet Frieze. Open: Tues., Wed., Fri. 10−16 hours, Thurs. 10−18 hours, Sun. 10−13 hours. Closed Mondays and Saturdays.

SMOCK:
Modeschule der Stadt Wien (Vienna Fashion School), XII., 79 Hetzendorfer Strasse (see plan p. I/22 below). By appointment tel. 84 27 95.

LITERATURE:
Nebehay, Ch. M.: Klimt-Dokumentation. Vienna 1969. (Pocketbook edition dtv 1146.1976). Novotny, Fritz − Dobai, Johannes: Gustav Klimt (Œuvre catalogue), Salzburg 1967. Strobl, Alice: Gustav Klimt, die Zeichnungen, 1878−1903; 1904−1911; in preparation, 1912−1918. Salzburg 1980−1984. Strobl, Alice: Zu den Fakultätsbildern von G. Klimt. Albertina-Studien, II, No 4, 1964.

EGON SCHIELE
1890–1918

EGON SCHIELE · 1890–1918

Egon Schiele (12 June 1890–31 October 1918) came of a good middle-class family that had no interest whatever in the arts. His grandfather Karl Ludwig Schiele (1817–1862) was born in Anhalt in Germany; he was a capable technician and built the railway line from Prague to Eger. He left the family his holdings in shares, which were burnt, in a fit of madness, by Schiele's father Adolf (1851–1905). (Adolf was, at the time, station master at Tulln, later to be retired for reasons of health.) From that day onward the family had only his scanty pension to live on and was practically reduced to poverty. Schiele suffered from the trauma of his father's early death just as Edvard Munch suffered from the deaths of his mother and his beloved sister. The atmosphere of melancholy, of autumn and decay that pervades his pictures —there is not a single drawing or portrait by him in which the features of the depicted are relaxed or happy—may be traced back to the mental strain caused by the illness and death of his father. Oddly enough, this applies only to his works of art: as a person he was said to have been gay and carefree, if a little careless. The notorious "Neulengbach Affair" very nearly ruined him. Even by modern standards the charges brought against him were weighty; he could count himself very lucky that they were eventually dropped. It is, indeed, a mistake to hold him up—as critics have been prone to do—as a victim of persecution and moralist prying. Schiele had the great good fortune to find buyers right from the start of his artistic career, even—and this is worth noting—when, in 1909 and within the space of a few months, he broke through to his own, expressionistic style. At the time of his death nearly all of his 300 paintings had been sold, thanks to a handful of enthusiasts who recognized his talent in good time and furthered it.

As far as women are concerned, we know only of his relationship with Wally Neuzil, who shared the ups and downs of his life until, in 1915, he left her abruptly and married Edith Harms. In contrast to Klimt, who was the lover of many of his models, Schiele would rather seem to have been an observer: obsessed, consumed by an inner flame. Those of his clients who bought his erotic works prompted him to be more and more daring. He made a living mostly from the sale of his drawings, which are all finished off, signed and dated.

When in 1915 he was called to arms, again a guardian angel stood by his side. Thanks to the indulgence of his superior officers, he was able to devote a part of his last years to his art. He was only 28 when he died in 1918. That year also saw the deaths of Gustav Klimt, Otto Wagner and Kolo Moser, thus depriving at one stroke the struggling young Austrian republic of its most distinguished artists.

Schiele—like Klimt—has only been rediscovered since the 1960s. His fame as one of the leading artists of our time is now firmly established.

Below (left to right): "Head I", rubber cut; "Mother holding up her baby", rubber cut; "Three men bathing", woodcut; "Head II", rubber cut. All done in Mühling in 1916 (Albertina).

The railway station at Tulln (photo taken about 1910), has remained practically unchanged to this day. Egon Schiele was born in the first-floor room with the double windows on the right. In 1901 he attended secondary school in Krems, and from 1902–1906 in Klosterneuburg, where the family joined him in 1904.

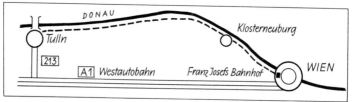

The parents with three children: on the left Egon, next to him Melanie (born 1886) and Elvira (died 1893). Gertrude (Gerti) was born in 1894.

Portrait of Schiele's mother. Black chalk. 1918. (Albertina).

Marie Schiele, née Soukup, born in Krumau, Bohemia, (1862–1935). Against the will of Egon's co-guardian, she managed to get him accepted at the Academy of Fine Arts in Vienna. Mother and son were not, however, always on the best of terms. Gertrude (Gerti) (1894–1982) who for a time was Schiele's favourite model, married his fellow student, the painter Anton Peschka (1885–1940).

Left: Gerti in front of the mirror in Schiele's studio, photograph around 1910.

Right: "Gerti in the nude". 1910. (Albertina).

Schiele was 16 when he was accepted at the Academy of Fine Arts, I., Schillerplatz. The nude class at the Academy. Photograph, around 1907. Egon Schiele is on the left next to the man with the hat.

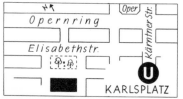

Professor Christian Griepenkerl (1839–1916), a teacher of the old school, was master of the drawing class Schiele attended for three years.

By 1907, Schiele, who had started painting landscapes at school in Klosterneuburg, had largely shaken off the academic traditions, as can be seen in his oil painting "Sailing boats on rippled water", Trieste 1907 (Neue Galerie, Graz, Styria).

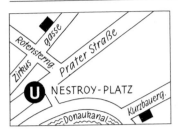

Schiele's first studio was at II., 6 Kurz-bauergasse, door 23. It was in Vienna's 2nd district that he first came across the city-bred proletariate, which he used as models for many of his drawings.

Leopold Czihaczek (1842–1929), Schiele's uncle and guardian, was Chief Inspector of the State Railways and a well-to-do man by his marriage to Schiele's aunt. He lived at II., 47 Zirkusgasse (now a council house) and was a lover of music; his nephew's activities were a mystery to him. The rupture came in May 1909: from that moment onwards Schiele had to fend for himself.

Left: Czihaczek's flat, oil, 1907 (Österr. Galerie).

Initially Schiele was influenced by the Secession, and especially by Gustav Klimt for whom he had a lifelong admiration.

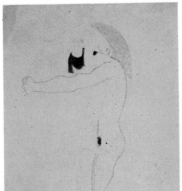

Right: "Lovers", coloured chalks, 1909 (Hist. Museum), shows the influence of Klimt's Beethoven Frieze.

"Portrait of Gertrude Schiele", oil, 1909 (Private collection, Vienna).

In 1909, within a few months, Schiele broke through to his own style. He was allowed to exhibit at the 2nd "Kunstschau" (Art Show) (Inner City Map No 8). His paintings there were hung next to those of Kokoschka who, being slightly touchy, took exception. The dreaded scandals—such as had given Klimt so much trouble—did not materialize: the public simply ignored the work of both the young artists.

Schiele left the Academy on 30th July, 1909 with the equivalent of a school certificate of maturity—a useful asset for his military service. He found a new studio at IX., 39 Alserbachstrasse (above), where he stayed until November 1910. Max Oppenheimer (1885–1954), painter and draughtsman, shared his studio with him for a while.

In December 1909 Gustav Pisko (above) generously put his premises at I., 14 Lothringerstrasse (Inner City Map No 13) at the disposal of the "New Artists", Schiele and his fellow students from the Academy. The most prominent among them were, apart from Schiele: Anton Faistauer (1887–1930); Franz Wiegele (1887–1944); Anton Peschka (1886–1940), who later became Schiele's brother-in-law; and Erwin Osen (1881–1970), painter of stage sets.

Arthur Roessler (1877–1955), critic and author, was Schiele's discoverer, friend and patron. Schiele made several portraits of him. The oil painting "Portrait of A. Roessler", 1910, is in the Hist. Museum.

Postcard from Krumau, written in Schiele's own hand, 15 May 1911: "This is the upper part of the 'Dead City'. Greetings, Egon Schiele (Stadtbibliothek).

From 1910 onward Egon Schiele travelled fairly often to Krumau near Budweis (České Bŭdějovice, Czechoslovakia), which was his mother's home town. In 1911 he lived there for a longer period. It was there that he painted—at first from nature—a series of his best townscapes; later his paintings were made up of different elements arbitrarily put together. His trip to Krumau in May 1910 in the company of Erwin Osen caused his uncle Leopold Czihaczek to lay down his co-guardianship of Schiele in a fit of anger, after having been fetched out of bed in the middle of the night to take delivery of a wrongly-addressed telegram in which Schiele asked for money.

"City and River", 1916 (Neue Galerie, Linz).

Around 1910 Schiele must have been very much under the influence of Erwin Osen, a rather eccentric character who was, among other things, a pantomime. It was only a short step from drawing Osen's gaunt body in the nude (above left; Neue Galerie, Graz) to drawing self-portraits, likewise in the nude (above right, Albertina).

The garden house in Krumau. Yielding to pressure from the town people, Schiele had to leave it in 1912, probably because of his "illicit" relationship with Wally Neuzil, but perhaps also because the house was much frequented by minors.

Schiele and Wally Neuzil (1894–1917) had lived together since 1911. When he married she was so disappointed that she volunteered as a Red Cross nurse in 1915 and died of scarlet fever in 1917 in a naval hospital at Sinj in Dalmatia.

 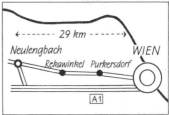

From mid-August 1911 (after his return from Krumau Schiele stayed temporarily with his mother at IX., 14/16 Sobieskigasse) until his arrest in April 1912, Schiele lived with Wally Neuzil at 48 Au in Neulengbach, Lower Austria (above). The house has remained almost unaltered.

Wally Neuzil, probably photographed by Roessler (Hist. Museum).

"Schiele's apartment in Neulengbach", oil, 1912. Strongly influenced by van Gogh, some of whose paintings had been on exhibit at the "Kunstschau" (Art Show) of 1909 (Hist. Museum).

County court, Neulengbach, 2 Hauptplatz. Schiele spent three weeks here pending trial. His cell (recognizable from the monogram that appears in one of his Neulengbach drawings) has since been converted into a coal cellar.

Schiele was arrested on 13 April 1912. He was charged with abduction of a girl still a minor (this charge was dropped); sexual relations with a girl still a minor (dropped in the course of the trial which took place in St. Pölten); and display of an erotic drawing in a room open to children. On this last charge he was sentenced to three days' arrest, which he had already served in the course of his three weeks' remand.

He felt that his very existence was at stake, and in a series of watercolours and drawings (Albertina) he took leave of those who were near and dear to him. He gave all these works dramatic captions: "I feel cleansed, not punished" (below left), and "For the sake of my art and my loved ones, I shall hold on" (below right).

After living for a short time with his mother (XII., 9 Rosenhügel-strasse), Schiele moved into Osen's former studio at IX., 18 Höfergasse, in July 1912 (above). In October 1912 he moved to the studio at XIII., 101 Hietzinger Hauptstrasse, in an elegant neighbourhood, which was to be his home until his death (below).

Gustav Klimt introduced Schiele to his patron, August Lederer. From then on his finances improved. Lederer invited him to Györ (Raab) in Hungary for Christmas/New Year 1912/13. He drew the members of the family and painted a portrait of the son Eric, with whom he became friends.

Egon Schiele in front of the big mirror in the studio in Hietzing, 1915.

"Portrait of Franz Hauer", dry-point etching (Albertina).

At A. Roessler's instigation Schiele began to do etchings in 1914, but soon lost interest. Franz Hauer (1866—1914), the proprietor of the restaurant "Griechenbeisl" at I., 11 Fleischmarkt, became one of Schiele's most important patrons. He owned over 1000 paintings by modern artists.

Schiele, whose weak constitution had absolved him from peacetime military service, appeared to be unmoved by the outbreak of the First World War; nor did it leave any traces in his art.

A special issue of the periodical "Der Ruf" had appeared in 1912. The title-page was designed after Schiele's self-portrait of 1910 (Albertina).

It seems strange that Schiele should have embarked on art photography in such turbulent times. He had already photographed in his adolescence; but now two of his artist friends, Anton Josef Trčka (alias Antios), painter, artisan and poet (1893–1940), and his neighbour in Hietzing, Johannes Fischer (1888–1955), painter and natural scientist, made several remarkable photographs of him. (Albertina, Egon Schiele Archives).

Schiele in his studio (below). As soon as he was better off, he started collecting works of art.

It can be assumed that Schiele produced several thousand drawings in the course of his life. As he lived mostly from the sale of
those drawings, he saw to it that they were properly finished off,
signed and dated. We have it from eyewitnesses that he took
barely more than ten minutes to complete a charcoal portrait. His
stroke is incredibly sure; corrections, even the slightest, are a
rarity. It is worth noting that in all his coveted coloured drawings
the wash was, without exception, added later. Some of his finest
drawings were executed in 1915, in what little free time he could
spare from his military duties (all Albertina).

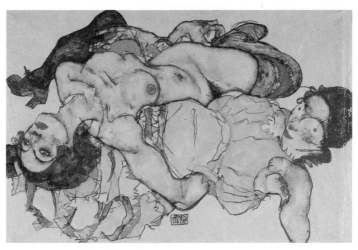

The poster, drawn by Schiele himself, for his exhibition at Guido Arnot's gallery at I., 15 Kärntnerring, 1ˢᵗ floor; no longer extant; Inner City Map No 14. (Hist. Museum).

After flirting with two girls from the house across the road at XIII., 114 Hietzinger Hauptstrasse (see map page II/14), he fell in love with one of them, Edith Harms, and married her. She came from just those middle-class circles that he had hoped to have left behind forever when he walked out of the Czihaczek home.

"Portrait of Edith Schiele", 1917/18 (Österr. Galerie)—the first of his paintings to be acquired by an Austrian museum. (The skirt, originally painted in coloured squares, had to be overpainted grey at the request of the then director of the museum, Hofrat

Haberditzl). At first Edith was his only model, but after a while professional models re-appeared. In June 1915 Schiele reported for military duty in Prague. After a short period of training in Bohemia he was transferred in August 1915 to Vienna, where he dug trenches in the deer park at Lainz and escorted Russian prisoners-of-war to and fro between Gänserndorf and Vienna.

Schiele as soldier (centre) with two colleagues. In March 1916 he was transferred to Mühling, near Wieselburg, where he worked as a clerk in a prisoner-of-war camp for Russian officers.

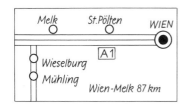

As in all his army posts he was lucky with his superior officers. His duties left him, however, little free time, so that in 1916 he produced only 8 oil paintings. On the whole this country job did him good, especially as the food was so much better. He also had Edith living in the neighbourhood. But he aimed at being transferred back to Vienna and roped all his friends and acquaintances in to help him in his endeavour. Below: "Watermill in Ruins" (on the river Erlauf), 1916 (N.Ö. Landes-Museum).

Karl Grünwald, charcoal, 1917 (Hist. Museum).

From January 1917 onward Schiele was, at last, in Vienna, working at the "supply stores for paid forces in the field", VI., 134 Mariahilfer Strasse. First Lieut. Karl Grünwald, an art dealer in civil life, and Dr. Hans von Rosé were his superior officers. Schiele was commissioned to draw depots in Vienna, Tyrol and South Tyrol for a calendar to be printed. For this calendar he also drew Grünwald's desk (below; private collection, London).

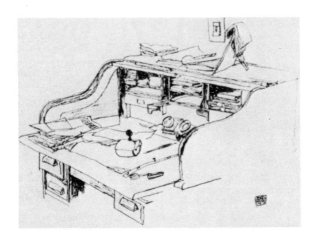

"Portrait of Hofrat Dr. Franz Martin Haberditzl", oil, 1917 (Private collection, Vienna). He is holding one of Schiele's fine sun flower drawings.

Schiele's meeting, in 1917, with Hofrat Haberditzl, director of the "Österreichische Galerie" (Inner City Map No 10), was of vital importance to him. This excellent museum official was the founder of the Austrian Baroque Museum in the Lower Belvedere. For the "Österreichische Galerie" he acquired the "Portrait of Edith Schiele" (see p.II/18), and had his own portrait drawn and painted by Schiele. Below: "Embrace", oil, 1917 (Österr. Galerie).

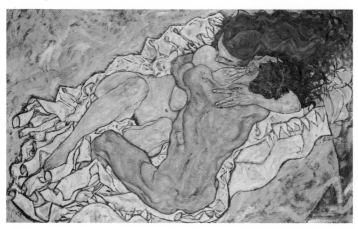

Schiele drew the poster for the Secession's 49th exhibition (Albertina). The exhibition (see Inner City Map No 21) was a great financial success for him: he earned 16,000 Kronen—a considerable sum even though the currency had already lost some of its purchasing power.

"The Family", oil, 1918, is Egon Schiele's last important painting. It was presumably inspired by Edith's pregnancy, although the mother in the picture does not resemble her (Österr. Galerie).

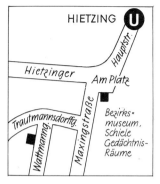

In August 1918 Schiele, who was now employed in the Army Museum in Vienna and had a good deal of free time at his disposal, moved into a new but damp studio at XIII., 6 Wattmanngasse. In the old studio in Hietzing he had wanted—as has lately become known—to start up a school for painting.

Edith Schiele, six months with child, died in Wattmanngasse on October 28th of the Spanish 'flu. Egon, who was the next victim, was transferred to his mother-in-law's apartment at XIII., 114 Hietzinger Hauptstrasse (see map on p. II/14) and died there at 1 a.m. on October 31st.

Benjamin Ferenczy (1890–1967), a Hungarian sculptor, was commissioned by Schiele's friends, in 1928, to put up a tombstone over the grave at the Ober St. Veit cemetery (row 10, group B, 15/6).

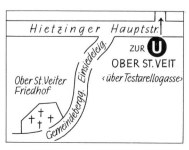

WHERE TO FIND:

PAINTINGS:
Österr. Gal. = Österreichische Galerie des 19. und 20. Jahrhunderts (Gallery of Austrian Art, 19th and 20th cent.), III., Oberes Belvedere (Inner City Map No 10). Open: Tues., Wed., Thurs., Sat. 10−16 hours, Fri. 10−13 hours, Sun. 9−12 hours. Closed on Mondays.

Mus. mod. Kunst = Museum moderner Kunst (Museum of Modern Art), Palais Liechtenstein, IX., 1 Fürstengasse (Inner City Map No 47). Open: Mon., Wed., Thurs., Fri., Sat., Sun. 10−18 hours. Closed on Tuesdays.

Neue Galerie am Steiermärkischen Landesmuseum Joanneum, Graz, Styria, 16 Sackstrasse. Open: Mon., Tues., Wed., Thurs., Fri. 10−18 hours, Sat., Sun. 10−13 hours.

Neue Galerie der Stadt Linz, Wolfgang-Gurlitt-Museum, Linz, Upper Austria, 15 Blütengasse. Open: Mon., Tues., Wed., Fri. 10−18 hours, Thurs. 10−22 hours, Sat. 10−13 hours. Closed on Sundays.

PAINTINGS AND EARLY DRAWINGS:
N.Ö. Landes-Mus. = Niederösterreichisches Landesmuseum (Lower Austrian County Museum), I., 9 Herrengasse (Inner City Map No 33). Open: Tues., Wed., Thurs., 9−17 hours, Sat. 9−14 hours, Sun. 9−12 hours. Closed on Mondays.

Hist. Mus. = Historisches Museum der Stadt Wien (City of Vienna Historical Museum), IV., Karlsplatz (Inner City Map No 15). Open: Tues., Wed., Fri. 10−16 hours, Thurs. 10−19 hours, Sat. 14−18 hours, Sun. 9−17 hours. Closed on Mondays.

DRAWINGS, LETTERS AND DOCUMENTS (EGON SCHIELE ARCHIVES BEQUEATHED BY MAX WAGNER):
Graphische Sammlung Albertina, I., 1 Augustinerstrasse (Inner City Map No 24), Printroom. Open: Mo., Tues., Wed., Thurs. 13−16 hours. Closed Fri.−Sun.

LETTERS:
Stadtbibliothek = Wiener Stadt- und Landesbibliothek (Library of the City of Vienna), I., Rathaus (Townhall) (Inner City Map No 30) Handschriftensammlung (Collection of Letters & Manuscripts). Open: Mo.−Thurs. 9−18,30 hours, Fri. 9−16,30 hours. Closed on Sat. and Sun.

EGON SCHIELE DOKUMENTATIONSZENTRUM AND MUSEUM (in preparation, to be opened 1984/5):
Internationale Schiele Gesellschaft, Tulln, N.Ö. (Lower Austria), 72 Donaulände, Bundesschulzentrum.

EGON SCHIELE MEMORIAL ROOM:
Heimatmuseum Hietzing (Museum devoted to the history of the XIIIth Viennese district) XIII., 2 Am Platz (see map p. II/23). Open: Sat. 14,30−17 hours, Sun. 10−12 hours.

EGON SCHIELE MEMORIAL PLAQUES:
XIII., 101 (studio) and 104 (where he died) Hietzinger Hauptstrasse (see map p. II/14).
II., 6 Kurzbauergasse (see map p. II/7). In preparation. Schiele's first studio.
Tulln, Lower Austria, Station (see map p. II/4). Here Schiele was born.

LITERATURE:
Ch. M. Nebehay: Egon Schiele, Leben, Briefe, Gedichte. Salzburg 1979.
Ch. M. Nebehay: Egon Schiele, Leben und Werk. Salzburg 1980 (Pocket edition: dtv Nr. 2884, 1983).

OSKAR KOKOSCHKA
1886–1980

OSKAR KOKOSCHKA · 1886−1980

Oskar Kokoschka (Pöchlarn an der Donau, March 1, 1886−Montreux, February 22, 1980) died at the age of 94. His life's work was gigantic: over 400 oil paintings (magnificent landscapes, first-rate portraits); over 500 graphic items; and innumerable drawings and water-colours. In his youth he designed postcards and posters; presented an Indian fairytale with self-made colour-slides; wrote dramas which were put to music by eminent composers; wrote a symbolic love story entitled "Die träumenden Knaben" (The dreaming boys); designed, in later years, stage sets for the Salzburg Festival; and taught there for years in his "Schule des Sehens" (School of Vision). He worked to the last, a Grand Old Man at the hub of the art scene.

He did not have an easy youth. His father, who had done badly in business, was unstable and restless. His mother, so he claimed, had had second sight; she probably passed her gift on to her son. His younger brother Bohuslav (1892−1976), also a painter, was overshadowed by him; a sister, Bertha, was married and lived in Prague, his father's native city. The family lived in straitened circumstances in Vienna and frequently changed addresses. After preparatory school Kokoschka went to secondary school at XVI., 7 Schuhmeierplatz. For a time he thought of studying chemistry; but his drawing master, Professor Schober, recognized his talent and helped him win a scholarship to the Academy of Applied Arts, which he attended from 1905 to 1909. (In 1911 he returned there as assistant teacher.)

Kokoschka spent his first ten creative years (1906−1915) in Vienna. His studio was at XIX., 27 Hardtgasse; it was painted black in

order−so he said−that the colours of his pictures should stand out better. It was here that he painted his famous "Die Windsbraut" (The tempest) 1914. As with Schiele, there came a break in his work: about 1908−practically overnight−he dropped everything he had been taught until then, cast off all influences, and broke through to a new and personal style. This first period in Vienna was one of the most important in his life and came to an end when in 1915 he was severely wounded in combat. In later years he visited Vienna only sporadically and worked either in his mother's house at XVI., 29 Liebhartstalstrasse, or in the homes of his portrait sitters.

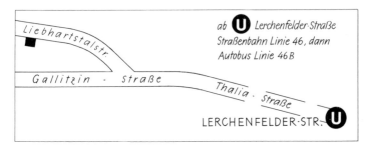

He was never on a good footing with Vienna. The reason why is not immediately apparent: admittedly, he was held up to ridicule, which must have been unbearable for so thin-skinned and unforgiving an artist. But what about Klimt, whose masterpieces were scoffed at each time they were exhibited? The public of those days was not ready for Kokoschka's art which (contrary to Klimt's) was beyond their understanding; so they just shook their heads and passed on. It would be a mistake, however, to think that he met only with criticism in Vienna: Adolf Loos was a lifelong friend of his and an appreciative patron who procured him numerous commissions (for which, as Kokoschka himself admits, he gave him small thanks). And Klimt? When the 1908 "Kunstschau" opened, he said: "Oskar Kokoschka is the most gifted of our young painters. Even if we were to run the risk of having our "Kunstschau" demolished—well then, let it be; but we have done our duty . . .".

Below: Oskar Kokoschka, Diary for huntsmen, 1907.

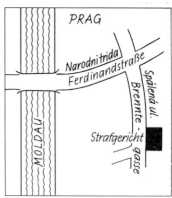

The father, Gustav Kokoschka
(1840–1923), Photograph.

Kokoschka and his father (Prague 1840–Vienna 1923) were not on particularly good terms. The father had learned the goldsmith's trade in his own father's prosperous shop in the Brenntegasse in Prague, but later quit to become a travelling salesman for a jewelry firm, which entailed long absences from his home and family. He gave his son books and a magic lantern to which the boy became particularly attached; but the worse he did in business, the more morose and reserved he became.

Gustav Kokoschka, Lithograph,
1918 (Albertina).

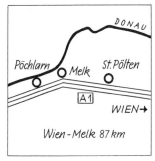

Kokoschka's birthplace in Pöchlarn, Lower Austria, today Kokoschka Documentary Centre.

Kokoschka was closer to his mother than to his father. A forester's daughter, she came from a large family and was born on September 27th 1861 in Hollenstein an der Ybbs, Lower Austria. Although she lived in Vienna, she gave birth to her son Oskar in the home of one of her brothers who owned a sawmill in Pöchlarn. She died on July 4th 1934 in Vienna. In the house where Kokoschka was born – 29 Regensburger Strasse, Pöchlarn – a Kokoschka documentary centre was set up in 1973.

Romana Kokoschka, née Loidl (the artist's mother). Lithograph, 1917 (Albertina).

Above: The nude class at the Kunstgewerbeschule, I., 10/2 Oskar-Kokoschka-Platz. Kokoschka is second from right.

From 1904—1909 Kokoschka attended the Kunstgewerbeschule. His teachers included C. O. Czeschka (1878—1960), Bertold Löffler (1874—1960), Erich Mallina (1873—1954) and Anton von Kenner (1871—1951). Of these, the most important for him were Czeschka and—after the latter's departure in 1907—his successor Löffler. His fellow students included Franz Karl Delavilla, Josef von Diveky, Urban Janke, Moriz Jung, Karl Schwetz, Fritz Weninger and Rudolf Kalvach. Kalvach's distinctive style influenced Kokoschka in those early years. Thanks to the excellent and progressive men who were teaching at the school at the time, the arts—and particularly the graphic arts—flourished as never before. The archives of the former Kunstgewerbeschule (later "Akademie" and now "Hochschule für angewandte Kunst", I., 2 Oskar-Kokoschka-Platz) house important documents and works of its students, including Kokoschka.

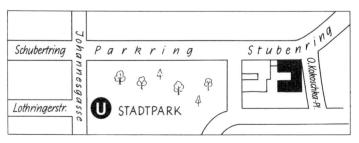

Carl Otto Czeschka (Vienna 1878—Hamburg 1960), one of Kokoschka's teachers, studied from 1894 to 1899 with Christian Griepenkerl (subsequently to be Egon Schiele's severe instructor) at the Academy. From 1902 to 1907 he taught at the Kunstgewerbeschule, and from 1907 to 1943 at the same institute in Hamburg. He was a first-rate teacher and an excellent illustrator, stage set designer and artisan. He did a lot of designing for the "Wiener Werkstätte".

Carl Otto Czeschka, cover for the first Fledermaus Cabaret programme. 1907 (Hist. Museum).

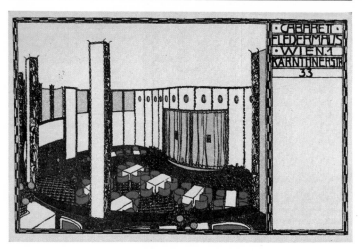

"Auditorium of the Fledermaus Cabaret", WW postcard No 139. Design by Josef Hoffmann (Hist. Museum).

Kokoschka worked for the legendary Fledermaus Cabaret, founded by the "Wiener Werkstätte", I., 33 Kärntnerstrasse, corner of Johannesgasse (Inner City Map No 45) (not preserved). ". . . (he) once showed his Indian fairytale "The Speckled Egg" with slides . . . Kokoschka himself was handling the projector with his unsteady hands, so that the effect was jerky, and the people started to laugh and make jokes and even complain. The whole thing was a failure." (Max Mell).

Kokoschka, "Stag, Fox and Shepherd". Coloured lithograph for his fairytale "The Speckled Egg". One of the illustrations to the programme for the opening of the Fledermaus Cabaret, 1907 (Hist. Museum).

The "Dreaming Boys" was Kokoschka's first work as a writer, illustrated by himself and published in 1908 under the imprint of the "Wiener Werkstätte" (Hist. Museum). His Indian ink drawings were presumably first coloured, and then transferred to the stones. An edition of 500 was printed, but it sold badly and was remaindered to the Kurt Wolf Verlag in Leipzig, which bought up 275 copies. The "Wiener Werkstätte" originally intended the book to be for children, but Kokoschka wrote an obscure text about his love for a Norwegian girl called Li. His drawings complement the text but do not actually illustrate it. The text was set to music in 1973 by Gottfried von Einem.

Kokoschka's first printed work—the picture sheet "Der Affe und der Papagei" ("The Monkey and the Parrot")—was published by the WW as one of a series of 18 colour-lithographs created by collaborators of the WW.

From 1906 to 1908 Kokoschka designed 15 coloured postcards (left: No 55; right: No 79) for the "Wiener Werkstätte", an arts and crafts association aiming at giving new impulses to art in all its ramifications. Altogether, more than 1000 "WW" postcards were published, of which 15 were by Kokoschka and 3 by Schiele.

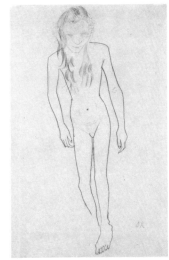

Left: Mother with child, about 1909 (Hist. Museum).
Right: Girl with long hair, about 1908.

Kokoschka's early drawings—most of them with wash—are clearly influenced by the Belgian sculptor George Minne (1866—1941), who had been shown by the Secession in Vienna. They also demonstrate his emancipation from the brightly coloured, decorative style of his work for the "Wiener Werkstätte". The breakthrough to his own style took place in 1907/08.

In 1898 George Minne (1866—1941) created a fountain with five kneeling boys (one of which is in the Museum moderner Kunst, Inner City Map No 47). It had considerable influence on both Kokoschka and Schiele. Both the Belgian Minne and the Swiss painter Ferdinand Hodler (1853—1918) owed the beginnings of their European reputation to the exhibitions of the Vienna Secession.

Kokoschka had his first exhibition at the legendary "Kunstschau". This art show was organized by the "Klimt group" after their departure from the Secession in 1905 and took place in a makeshift exhibition building on the grounds of the present Konzerthaus (Inner City Map No 8). Kokoschka designed the poster for the show (left; Hist. Museum).

A new "Kunstschau" was put on in 1909. Kokoschka's play "Mörder, Hoffnung der Frauen" ("Murderer, Hope of Women") saw its first performance in the garden theatre and was set to music by Paul Hindemith in 1921. Below right: Kokoschka's poster for his play (Hist. Museum). Herwarth Walden invited Kokoschka to Berlin in 1910 and published the drawing in his periodical "Der Sturm" (left).

"Der Trancespieler" (The Trance Actor), 1908 (Musées Royaux des Beaux Arts, Brussels).

The actor Ernst Reinhold played the lead in and directed Kokoschka's play "Mörder, Hoffnung der Frauen". Kokoschka named his portrait "The Trance Actor", ". . . because I had thoughts about him that I could not express in words . . .".

Kokoschka (left) and Ernst Reinhold (right). Seated in front: Max Oppenheimer ("Mopp"; 1885–1954), painter and graphic artist, who used to be on close terms with Egon Schiele. Photograph, about 1910 (Hist. Museum).

"Der Rentmeister" (probably a Viennese appraiser), about 1911 (Österr. Gal.).

"Alter Mann" (Old Man, Hirsch senior). Painted in 1906, after Kokoschka had paid a visit to a van Gogh exhibition in Vienna (Neue Galerie, Linz).

At 21 years of age Kokoschka was already a master of the art of portraiture. He got behind the façade of his sitters and showed up their anxieties and vulnerability.

"Portrait of Adolf Loos", 1909 (Nationalgalerie, Berlin).

For Kokoschka the meeting with architect Adolf Loos (1870–1933), the uncompromising pioneer of functional, unadorned building, was of prime importance; for it was Loos who loosened his ties with the "Wiener Werkstätte" group, procured him commissions and persuaded him to go to Berlin in 1910. Loos possessed a number of drawings and no less than 26 paintings by Kokoschka who, in the choice of his models, showed a strange inclination towards the darker aspects of human nature. It was Loos, too, who put Kokoschka in touch with two institutes that were to be of great importance to him: the "Akademischer Verband für Literatur und Musik in Wien" ("Academic Association for Literature and Music in Vienna"); and the group surrounding Eugenie Schwarzwald, at whose private school Kokoschka taught drawing for a short time.

Peter Altenberg (alias Richard Engländer; 1859—1919) was a master of impressionistic prose, a bohémien with whom Loos spent many a night in the bars of Vienna. 1909. (Private collection, New York).

The photograph below shows Kokoschka (centre left) with author and social historian Egon Friedell (1878—1938) and Peter Altenberg (centre right) on the Semmering, a summer resort south of Vienna frequented by many Viennese artists (including Adolf Loos).

Portrait of Karl Kraus. Pen, ink and wash. About 1909. (Private collection, Switzerland).

Karl Kraus (1874–1936), author, from 1899 on editor of "Die Fackel" (The Torch), a belligerent, highly controversial periodical. His command of language and his wit made him one of the greatest satirists in the German tongue.

Karl Kraus was a friend of Adolf Loos's. He rediscovered Johann Nestroy for the public and furthered Peter Altenberg, Else Laske-Schüler, Georg Trakl and Arnold Schönberg. He was also on a friendly footing with Kokoschka.

Portrait of Karl Kraus, 1908, Photograph by Madame d'Ora (Dora Kallmus).

"Still life with sheep and hyacinth", 1909 (Österr. Galerie). In his autobiography Kokoschka writes that he was commissioned to paint a portrait of the son of the art collector Dr. Oskar Reichel ("Boy with raised hand", 1909). He found the gutted sheep in the kitchen and painted it, together with the boy's aquarium (reproduction erroneously reversed).

"Dents du Midi" (painted from Leysin where Loos had taken him), 1909/10. (Private collection, Zürich). This is one of the first of his masterly landscapes.

"Die Windsbraut" (The Tempest), 1914. (Art Museum, Basel). It was the poet Georg Trakl (1887–1914) who devised the title during a visit to Kokoschka's "black" studio (see map p. III/2). The painting may be interpreted as an epilogue to his wild love affair with Alma Mahler.

Alma Mahler (1879–1964), wearing jewelry designed by Kolo Moser. Photograph, 1904. The daughter of the painter Emil Schindler and stepdaughter of the painter Carl Moll, she was married three times: to Gustav Mahler, Walter Gropius and Franz Werfel. A love affair with Gustav Klimt was nipped in the bud by Moll.

Carl Moll (1861—1945), painter. Stepfather of Alma Mahler-Werfel. 1913/14 (Österr. Galerie).

Carl Moll, a man of taste and artistic accomplishment, was one of the trend-setters of the Viennese art scene, renowned as a promoter of important exhibitions. In 1897 he became a founding member of the Secession. It was on account of his activities on behalf of the Galerie Miethke that the Klimt group walked out of the Secession in 1905. Josef Hoffmann built him two houses. In 1945, when the Russians marched into Vienna, he, his daughter Marie and his son-in-law committed suicide.

From 1913 on Kokoschka realized the possibilities—both artistic and commercial—of lithography. In his cycles "Die Chinesische Mauer" (The Chinese Wall), "Der gefesselte Kolumbus" (Columbus enchained) and "O Ewigkeit Du Donnerwort" (Eternity Thou Thunderous Voice) he used to the full the graphic skills he had acquired up to then.

Above left: "At the Spinning Wheel", one of the eight lithographs illustrating Karl Kraus' story "The Chinese Wall". 1913/14.

Above right: "Eve's Apple", one of the twelve lithographs illustrating Kokoschka's story "Columbus enchained". Alma Mahler sat as model. 1916–21.

Left: "Self-portrait". (Head and shoulders, holding a pencil). One of the eleven lithographs illustrating: "O Ewigkeit Du Donnerwort" (Eternity Thou Thunderous Voice) by J. S. Bach. 1916–1918.

"Oskar Kokoschka as volunteer with the 15th Imperial Royal Dragoons". Photograph by H. Schieberth, Vienna, 1915 (Hist. Museum).

Loos had succeeded in getting his protégé enrolled in one of the monarchy's most distinguished regiments. Of the major Austrian artists, he was the only one who went to the front. On 29th August 1915 he was severely wounded: a bullet had penetrated his skull and was removed in the army emergency hospital in the Palais Palffy, I., Josefsplatz. The bullet is on show in the Kokoschka Documentary Centre at Pöchlarn. Kokoschka felt the effects of his war wound for a long time afterwards. The brilliant years of his Viennese beginnings had drawn to a close.

"Wien, vom Wilhelminenberg gesehen" (Vienna seen from a hill in the XVIth district), 1931. (Hist. Museum).

In 1917 Kokoschka left Vienna for Dresden. From then on he only paid sporadic visits to Vienna. He spent the summer of 1931 in his mother's house in the Liebhartstal (see map p. III/3). The City Council commissioned him to paint a view of Vienna, and he chose the outlook from the Wilhelminenberg (above). The castle had at that time been taken over by a children's home run by the City of Vienna. Kokoschka took this as a challenge: "It was my first painting with a political content", he wrote later. Oddly enough, the City Council hesitated, at first, to accept the painting. In 1956 Kokoschka—now world-renowned—painted the Vienna Opera, which had been re-opened in 1955 (below).

The final reconciliation with Vienna came when the City put on the great Kokoschka retrospective exhibition on the occasion of his 85th birthday.

"Die Wiener Staatsoper" (The State Opera, Vienna), 1956. (Österr. Gal.).

WHERE TO FIND:

PAINTINGS:
Österr. Galerie = Österreichische Galerie des 19. und 20. Jahrhunderts (Gallery of Austrian Art, 19th and 20th cent.), III, Oberes Belvedere (Inner City Map No 10). Open: Tues., Wed., Thurs., Sat. 10–16 hours, Fri. 10–13 hours, Sun. 9–12 hours. Closed on Mondays.

Hist. Museum = Historisches Museum der Stadt Wien (City of Vienna Historical Museum), IV., Karlsplatz (Inner City Map No 15). Open: Tues., Wed., Fri. 10–16 hours, Thurs. 10–19 hours, Sat. 14–18 hours, Sun. 9–17 hours. Closed on Mondays.

Mus. mod. Kunst = Museum moderner Kunst (Museum of Modern Art), Palais Liechtenstein, IX., 1 Fürstengasse (Inner City Map No 47). Open: Mon., Wed., Thurs., Fri., Sat., Sun. 10–18 hours. Closed on Tuesdays.

Neue Galerie der Stadt Linz, Wolfgang-Gurlitt-Museum, Linz, Upper Austria, 15 Blütengasse. Open: Mon., Tues., Wed., Fri. 10–18 hours, Thurs. 10–22 hours, Sat. 10–13 hours. Closed on Sundays.

GRAPHICS AND DRAWINGS:
Albertina = Graphische Sammlung Albertina, I., 1 Augustinerstrasse (Inner City Map No 24), Printroom. Open: Mo., Tues., Wed., Thurs. 13–16 hours. Closed Fri–Sun.

GRAPHICS, PHOTOGRAPHS, POSTERS, DRAWINGS:
Hist. Museum (see above).

Hochschule ang. Kunst = Hochschule für angewandte Kunst (Academy of Applied Arts), I., 2 Oskar-Kokoschka-Platz (Inner City Map No 2), library and archives. Open: Mo.–Fri. 9–16 hours.

Salzburger Landessammlung Rupertinum (Rupertinum), 9 Wiener Philharmonikerstrasse, Salzburg, Friedrich Welz Bequest. Open: daily 10–17 hours.

DOCUMENTATION:
Oskar-Kokoschka-Dokumentation, Pöchlarn, Lower Austria, 29 Regensburger Strasse. Open in the summer: Wed.–Sun. 10–12 and 14–17 hours. Enquiries: Johann Winkler, Tel. Vienna (0222) 4300/2698.

Literature:
Der frühe Kokoschka. Ausstellungskatalog, Hist. Museum der Stadt Wien, 1982.
O. Kokoschka: Mein Leben, München 1973.
Schweiger, Werner J.: Wiener Werkstätte. Kunst und Handwerk 1903–1932. Wien 1982.
Schweiger, Werner J.: Der junge Kokoschka, Leben und Werk. 1904–1914. Wien 1983.
Wingler, Hans M.: Oskar Kokoschka. Das Werk. Salzburg 1951.
Wingler, Hans M.; Welz, Friedrich: Oskar Kokoschka. Das graphische Werk. Salzburg 1975.

Below: Oskar Kokoschka, Diary for huntsmen, 1907

OTTO WAGNER
1841–1918

"Artis sola domina necessitas"
(Art knows only one master: necessity).
Motto of Gustav Semper, taken over by Otto Wagner.

Otto Wagner (July 13, 1841–April 10, 1918), son of a Viennese notary, Rudolf Simeon Wagner (1802–1846), came of good bourgeois stock. After attending the Akademisches Gymnasium in Vienna and the boarding-school of the Benedictine monks in Melk, he went to the Vienna Polytechnic Institute (now Technical University) from 1857 to 1859, to the Berlin Royal School of Architecture from 1860 to 1861, and to the Vienna Academy (under van der Nüll and Sicardsburg) from 1861 to 1863. Finally he worked for a year in the studio of the planner of the Ringstrasse, the late Ludwig von Förster (1797–1863).

Wagner was the 'grand seigneur' among the Viennese architects of his time. Although he had his roots firmly in the 19th century, he nevertheless had an eye for the future. His façades range from historicism through the Secession style to modern functionalism. All his buildings are practical, most of them are exemplary. He was open to the use of modern construction methods (steel skeleton) and of new materials (the Majolica House; thin marble slabs for the façade of the Postsparkasse/Post Office Savings Bank), used aluminium to decorate his buildings (Post Office Savings Bank, Steinhof church); and built business houses with projecting windows on the ground and mezzanine floors (Anker House, 1895). He was a man of bold enterprise, building his houses according to his own ideas at his own expense and then selling them, in finished form, to others. He acquired extensive sites on which he usually put up several buildings. As he kept no records, many of his earlier constructions are unknown; some have been destroyed. Many of his ambitious and important projects were not executed: the new Academy of Arts, 1898; the renovation of the Capuchin church, 1898; the City Museum, 1901–1914; a hotel on the Ringstrasse, 1910; the University Library, 1914, etc. The outbreak of the First World War prevented him from working as city planner of Sydney. Berta Zuckerkandl handed down to us a remark made by Gustav Klimt to Otto Wagner: "They won't let you build the walls on which they won't let me paint my friezes." He joined the Vienna Secession in 1899 and maintained friendly relations with the Klimt group until his death. He also helped Egon Schiele when he was young. Almost all the important Viennese architects were his pupils at the Vienna Academy, where he succeeded Hasenauer and taught from 1884 to 1913: Joseph Maria Olbrich, Josef Hoffmann (who said: "We who had the good fortune to stand at his side and who honoured him as a master and a pioneer, sometimes even as a friend, are

above all grateful to him for the countless impulses he gave us."),
Jan Kŏtera (founder of the Czech Society of Arts and Crafts), Josef
Plečnik, Marcel Kammerer, Otto Schönthal, Emil Hoppe, Ernst
Lichtblau, Max Fabiani—to name only a few—were among his
disciples.

Otto Wagner's first wife was Josefine Domhart. In 1880 he
divorced her and married, in 1881, Luise Stiffel (1859–1915),
nearly 20 years his junior, with whom he lived happily for 34
years.

Below: Otto Wagner and colleagues, about 1898: J. M. Olbrich (first from left), J. Plečnik (second from right), behind him J. Hoffmann.

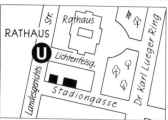

The façade of this early construction of Wagner's at I., 10 Stadiongasse (1888) still shows the influence of historicism—in this case the Italian Renaissance.

IV/4

The roof construction of this apartment house already bears Otto Wagner's personal stamp. Decorative work can be seen just under the upper cornice.

In 1886–1888 Wagner built himself a luxurious villa at XIII., 26 Hüttelbergstrasse. The site was somewhat remote and isolated, on a wooded slope and very shady. The lefthand pergola was extended in 1900 to form a studio, the righthand pergola in 1895 to form a sitting-room. Wagner sold the villa to Ben Tieber, music hall director and proprietor of the Ronacher Vaudeville Theatre. The present owner is the painter Ernst Fuchs, who added decoration of his own to the façade.

In 1890/91 Otto Wagner built his "town house" at III., 1 Rennweg, which, with its richly decorated façade, is a gem of the period. His studio was on the ground floor. Later he sold the house to Countess Hoyos; it is now the Yugoslav embassy. The neighbouring house at 3 Rennweg was also built by Wagner.

In order to be able to use the Danube Canal at low water level (it was planned to serve as a winter harbour) and to keep it free of ice, the Danube Regulation Commission built locks in 1894−1908. Wagner sat on the advisory committee. He remodelled the company building; in 1894/98 he built the Nussdorf lock (above) and in 1906/7 the charming "Schützenhaus der Staustufe Kaiserbad" (below), a lockhouse on the left bank opposite the present Underground station "Schottenring". As the lock was never put into action, the whole of the sophisticated apparatus (crane, etc.) was dismantled. The lockhouse has been preserved, a remarkable example of Wagner's late style.

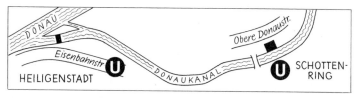

The City Railway bridge spanning the Wien river (between Subway stations Gumpendorfer Strasse and Meidlinger Hauptstrasse).

In 1892 a law was passed whereby the re-fashioning of the Danube Canal, the regulation of the river Wien and the construction of the "Stadtbahn" (City Railway) were all to be taken in hand simultaneously. The City Railway was steam-driven; it was built to conform with the military authorities' wish that it should connect all the main Viennese railway stations. The present-day Underground covers only a part of the former network: the "Vorortelinie" (suburban line) and "Verbindungsbahn" (junction line) have been practically out of use since the end of the First World War. The City Railway ran right round the Inner City; direct lines served the outlying districts, a convenience no longer available today.

For the City Railway's 40-kilometer network Wagner built 36 stations and all the bridges, cuttings and galleries: to quote Josef Hoffmann, ". . . the only ones of their kind that have not disfigured a city but, on the contrary, have created a series of the most attractive townscapes imaginable . . ." In our days the tracks of the old City Railway are being used by the Vienna Underground; many of Wagner's stations, however, have been pulled down or are in a bad state of repair.

A special station, built in front of Schönbrunn Castle for the private use of the Imperial family, was particularly richly decorated both outside and inside (below: carpet in the court waiting room). It is now in a regrettably bad state of repair.

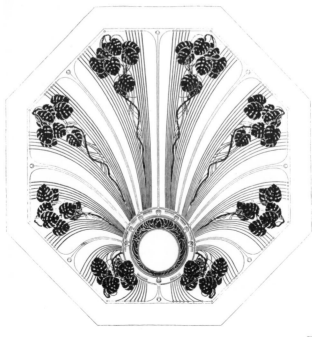

The two elegant Karlsplatz stations of the City Railway have been moved to another site and, excellently restored, made into an Otto Wagner Museum and a coffeehouse (Inner City Map No 17). With their rich ornamentation they outshine even the Paris Metro stations. Below: Entrance of the U-station "Stadtpark" (Inner City Map No 7).

The building of the insurance company "Der Anker" ("The Anchor") at I., corner of 10 Graben and 2 Spiegelgasse (Inner City Map No 39) was built in 1895. The glass superstructure was originally destined to be Wagner's studio; it was later turned into a photographer's studio and is now used by the painter Friedensreich Hundertwasser.

A noteworthy feature is the use of the "entresol" for business premises and its consequent separation from the residential floors above. This idea was taken up by Loos for his house on the Michaelerplatz.

The two apartment houses at VI., 38 and 40 Linke Wienzeile, illustrate Wagner's habit of building several houses in a row wherever possible. Built in 1898/99, they were recently painstakingly restored and reckon among the finest Jugendstil buildings in Vienna. Wagner gave the house on the left a practically indestructible façade—hence the name "Majolica House".

This photograph, taken while the building was under construction, gives a good idea of the Majolica House's impressive façade with its lovingly executed details. The windows have not yet been put in, nor is the scaffolding completely removed. On the right, No 38 can be seen in its completed state.

Staircase and lift cage at No 40. The entrance to No 38 is in 1 Köstlergasse (below).

Otto Wagner's project for the Austrian Post Office Savings Bank won the first prize over 36 contestants. The building, constructed in 1904—6 and 1910—12 (second phase), is a showpiece of modern architecture, a model of well conceived, functional detail. Regrettably, the hall was "modernized" some time ago.

Wagner struck a novel note with the façade which consisted of thin Sterzing marble slabs that were bolted together. Aluminium was used for the ornamentation as well as for the pipes (now no longer in use) that blew hot air into the rooms—a heating system that caused widespread interest at the time. The offices had sliding walls by means of which the space available could be changed at will. Wagner also designed the complete interior decoration.

Board room. Portrait of Emperor Francis Joseph I by Wilhelm List (1864–1918), painter and graphic artist, a co-founder of the Secession.

Note the furniture designed by Otto Wagner. The stool shown below is still in use.

The main hall (above).
One of the aluminium hot-air pipes in the main hall (below).

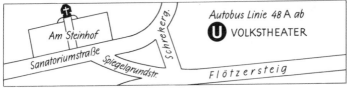

In 1902 Wagner had taken part in a competition for the construction of the Lower Austrian mental hospital at Steinhof, which was later taken over by the City of Vienna. His general layout was accepted, but not his plans for the individual pavilions. He did, however, design the famous church overlooking the western approach to Vienna, which brought him international fame. Both the church and the asylum were built between 1905 and 1907. The church was meant for the use of the quieter patients, and the pews were so spaced out as to allow the supervisors to intervene without difficulty. The glass windows were designed by Kolo Moser (1868–1918). The famous cupola is roofed with (originally gilded) copper plating.

View of the high altar from the choir. The mosaic work in majolicà, marble, enamel and glass, designed by Remigius Geyling (1878–1974), was only completed in 1913.

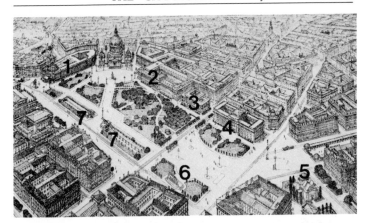

Otto Wagner's project for the Karlsplatz, 1909 (above).
1) Project for an "Emperor Francis Joseph Museum" (City Museum) – 2) Technical University – 3) Protestant school – 4) Project for a department store – 5) The Secession building – 6) Project for a monumental fountain – 7) City Railway station at the Karlsplatz.

Wagner fought for his "City Museum" project for thirteen years in vain. First he was defeated by Friedrich Schachner (1841–1907), favoured by the "Künstlerhaus", later Count Karl Lanckorónski (1848–1933) collector, art patron and implacable enemy of all things modern, killed Wagner's project by collecting signatures against it. Another project on the "Schmelz" (in the 15th district) was stopped by the outbreak of the First World War in 1914.

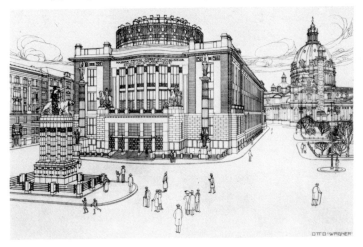

"Leprosy Sanatorium", entrance. 1910–13. Now Pavilion 24 of the Wilhelminen-Hospital, XVI., 37 Montleartstrasse (above).

Both the Leprosy Sanatorium and Wagner's second villa at XIII., 28 Hüttelbergstrasse (see map p. IV/6) bear marks of Wagner's late style, i.e. smooth surfaces and little ornamentation.

Apartment house at VII., 4 Döblergasse, adjoining 40 Neustiftgasse. Both houses were built by Wagner between 1909 and 1912. Wagner had an apartment and his last studio at 4 Döblergasse.

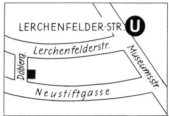

Otto Wagner's apartment at VII., 4 Döblergasse. In contrast to his late façades, Wagner's interiors were still over-elaborate. The apartment still exists. Damaged or missing elements (fittings, glass doors and lighting) have been replaced; but there is very little left of the original furniture. There are plans to turn the apartment into an Otto Wagner museum.

Below: Dining room in Wagner's apartment; photograph, 1913.

WHERE TO FIND:

BUILDINGS (see also in text):
Österreichische Postsparkasse (Post Office Savings Bank), I., Georg-Coch-Platz (Inner City Map No 1). Kassensaal (Main Hall). Open: Mon., Tues., Wed., Fri. 8–15 hours, Thurs. 8–17,30 hours. Closed on Saturdays and Sundays.

Kirche am Steinhof (Church at Steinhof). Psychiatrisches Krankenhaus der Stadt Wien (Psychiatric Clinic of the City of Vienna), XIV., Baumgartner Höhe (see map p. IV/19). For visits phone 94 84 845.

PHOTOS, POSTERS, PROJECTS, ETC.:
Historisches Museum der Stadt Wien (Historical Museum, City of Vienna), IV., Karlsplatz (see Inner City Map No 15). Open: Tues., Wed., Fri. 10–16 hours, Thurs. 10–19 hours, Sat. 14–18 hours, Sun. 9–17 hours, closed on Mondays. Otto Wagner Museum in the former Karlsplatz City Railway station building (see Inner City Map No 17). Open 1 April to 30 October at the above hours.

PLANS AND LITERATURE:
Akademie der bildenden Künste, I., 1 Schillerplatz (Inner City Map No 19). Bibliothek (Library) and Kupferstichkabinett (Print Room). Open: Tues., Thurs., Fri. 10–14 hours, Wed. 10–13,15–18 hours. Sat. and Sun. 9–13 hours. Closed on Mondays.

MEMORIALS:
Wagner Memorial designed by Josef Hoffmann, I., Makartgasse (Inner City Map No 20).
Wagner's grave, designed by himself (an early work). Hietzinger Friedhof/ Hietzing Cemetery, XIII., 15 Maxingstrasse, group 13, grave 131. Take Underground to Hietzing station. From there 10 minutes walk.

Literature:
Otto Wagner, Die Baukunst unserer Zeit. Reprint of the 4th edition of 1914, Vienna 1979.
Geretsegger, Heinz and Peintner, Max: Otto Wagner, Salzburg 1983[3].

JOSEPH MARIA OLBRICH
1867–1908

JOSEPH MARIA OLBRICH · 1867–1908

Joseph Maria Olbrich, son of Edmund Olbrich (1837–1902), house-owner and confectioner, was born in Troppau (now Opava, Czechoslovakia) on December 22nd, 1867 and died in Düsseldorf on August 8th, 1908. He was an architect, craftsman and painter. From 1882 to 1886 he attended the State Arts and Crafts College in Vienna; from 1890 to 1893 the Academy of Arts under Carl von Hasenauer and Otto Wagner; in 1893 Otto Wagner employed him as a draughtsman; he won the Rome Prize and travelled through Italy and North Africa from 1893 to 1894; went back to work with Otto Wagner in 1894; was a co-founder of the Secession in 1897; and in 1899–after an unsuccessful attempt by Wagner to get him a professorship in Vienna–the Grand Duke Ernst Ludwig of Hesse called him to Darmstadt to help found the artists' colony there. Olbrich turned out to be a pace-setter of the Modern Style in Germany. In Vienna he was active for only two years; nevertheless his Secession building is a major landmark in the development of 'Art Nouveau' architecture.

Ludwig Hevesi, art critic and chronicler of the Vienna Secession, writes: "He had the gay, winged phantasy, the innate distinction and the winning charm of a Schubert or a Johann Strauß. With his imaginative and decorative temperament, Olbrich was primarily a luxury artist . . . he became the most sought-after architect in West Germany. His ebullient inventiveness seemed to have no end. He divided his efforts between building and the applied arts: his jewel boxes, French clocks, caskets, all the delicate trinkets he improvised flooded the Christmas markets . . . Olbrich will be remembered in Vienna as one of the pioneers to whom we owe the immense significance of our epoch . . ."

"Ver Sacrum", the Secession's periodical, was the mouthpiece for the artists' progressive ideas. Olbrich's ornamental work is best studied in the issues of the first year, 1898. Below: Some of the illustrations (marginal ornaments and vignettes) that are scattered throughout the text. (Hist. Museum).

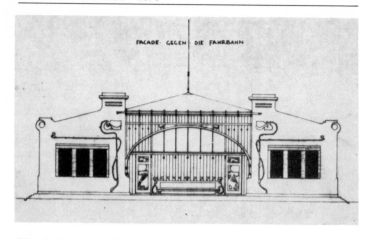

FACADE GEGEN DIE FAHRBAHN

Sketch for the clubhouse of the Civil Servants' Cycling Club, II., 7 Rustenschacher Allee, 1898 (now 'Sportclub Schwarz-Blau' and practically unaltered).

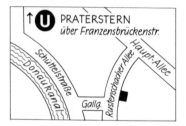

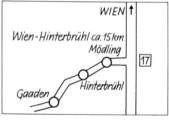

Villa Max Friedmann at 27 Hauptstrasse, Hinterbrühl, 1898. The style anticipates his later work on the Mathildenhöhe in Darmstadt. A salient feature is the ornamental staircase.

Olbrich's Secession building is one of the masterpieces of European "Jugendstil". Klimt was instrumental in toning down the original project, which was somewhat flamboyant. The building rests on concrete pillars brought down 25 ft. to the bed of the built-over Ottakring rivulet. The sliding walls inside the house allow for a varying arrangement of the rooms. The building costs of 60,000 gulden were largely borne by the artists themselves; those who worked on the building did so on a voluntary basis. The City of Vienna provided the site, but failed to honour all its promises: e. g., the avenue that should have connected the Secession with the Karlskirche did not materialize.

The bronze doors, by Georg Klimt, have been replaced by replicas. The interior of the house has been altered and, as a result, robbed of its superbly designed functionalism. This jewel of the "Jugendstil" era is not in a particularly good state of repair; the cupola needs re-gilding.

The wording over the entrance reads: "TO EACH AGE ITS ART, TO ART ITS FREEDOM" and was conceived by the critic Ludwig Hevesi. During the Third Reich, 1938–45, it was taken down. The cupola, consisting of intertwining leaves made of gilded bronze, was nicknamed "The Golden Cabbage".

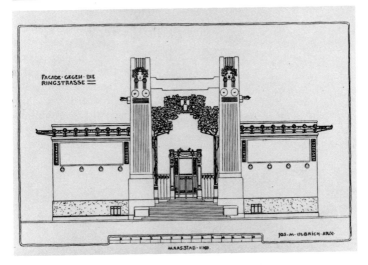

This very ornate sketch—still influenced by Otto Wagner—shows Olbrich on the quest for the final form. Note the two large surfaces intended to take frescoes or mosaics.

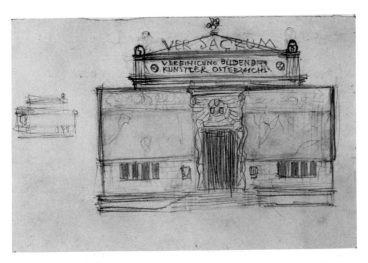

Gustav Klimt, as President of the Secession, intervened in favour of a more sober design and put his ideas on record in two drawings (Hist. Museum and private collection). It is interesting to note that he, too, had a decorative front elevation in mind.

V/7

Olbrich and Josef Hoffmann together designed the interior decoration for the 1st exhibition of the Secession on the premises of the Vienna Horticultural Society (Gartenbau-Gesellschaft; Inner City Map No 6), 1898.

Interior of the 4th exhibition, 18 February−31 May, 1899. In the foreground, the plaster model for "Marc Anthony" by Arthur Strasser (1854−1927). The original, in bronze, now stands next to the Secession.

Interior decoration for Hermann Bahr's house. Olbrich integrated Klimt's "Nuda Veritas", 1899 (today Theatersammlung, Österr. Nationalbibliothek) into the study.

Left: Cutlery, about 1900 (Mus. f. angew. Kunst). Right: chair, once property of the Viennese actress Maria Wölzl, about 1898/99 (private collection).

This house, built in 1899/1900 for Hermann Bahr (1863–1934), author and critic, at XIII., 22 Winzerstrasse, still exists, slightly altered. Bahr was the foremost champion of the new movement, a fact that earned him sharp criticism from Karl Kraus.

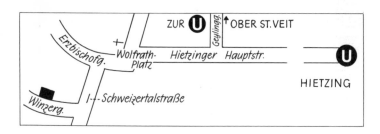

The house that Olbrich built in 1899 for Ernst Stöhr (1860–1917), painter, graphic artist, poet and musician, in his native town of St. Pölten in Lower Austria at 41 Kremsergasse, is still in good condition. Stöhr was the ideologist of the Secession: he was the first to recognize Klimt's importance in the Austrian art scene (catalogue of the 18th exhibition, 1903) and it was presumably he who laid down the programme for Gustav Klimt's "Beethoven Frieze".

St. Pölten   ←---------   62 km   ---------→   WIEN

A1   Westautobahn

WHERE TO FIND:

BUILDINGS (see also text):
Secession, I., 12 Friedrichstrasse (Inner City Map No 21). Open during exhibitions or by appointment, Telephone 57 53 07.

APPLIED ARTS:
Hist. Museum = Historisches Museum der Stadt Wien (City of Vienna Historical Museum), IV., Karlsplatz (Inner City Map No 15). Open: Tues., Wed., Fri. 10−16 hours, Thurs. 10−19 hours, Sat. 14−18 hours, Sun. 9−17 hours. Closed on Mondays.

Mus. f. angew. Kunst = Museum für angewandte Kunst (Museum of Applied Arts), I., 5 Stubenring (Inner City Map No 4). Open: Tues., Wed., Fri., 10−16 hours, Thurs. 10−18 hours, Sun. 10−13 hours. Closed on Mondays and Saturdays.

Theatersammlung = Theatersammlung der österreichischen Nationalbibliothek (Theatre Collection of the Austrian National Library), "Österreichisches Theatermuseum" (Austrian Theatre Museum). Anna Bahr-Mildenburg memorial room. Open: Tues., Thurs., 11 hours. Apply to "Kasse der Bundestheater" (Box-office of the State Theatres), I., 3 Hanuschgasse, near Albertina (Inner City Map No 24).

SKETCHES, DRAWINGS, PLANS:
Akademie der bildenden Künste (Academy of Fine Arts), I., 1 Schillerplatz (Inner City Map No 19), Library and Print-Room. Open: Tues., Thurs., Fri. 10−14 hours, Wed. 10−13 and 15−18 hours. Sat. and Sun. 9−13 hours. Closed on Mondays. On view there: the vols. of "Ver Sacrum"; Oblrich's book "Ideen" (Ideas), Introduction by Ludwig Hevesi, Vienna 1900, etc.

Literature:
Nebehay, Christian M., Ver Sacrum 1898−1903, Vienna 1982 (English edition published in London and New York).
Joseph Maria Olbrich, 1867−1908. Catalogue of an exhibition held on the occasion of his 100th anniversary, Darmstadt 1967.
Joseph Maria Olbrich, "Die Zeichnungen in der Kunstbibliothek Berlin" (The drawings in the 'Kunstbibliothek', Berlin). Critical catalogue, Berlin 1972.
Joseph Maria Olbrich, 1867−1908. Exhibition catalogue, Darmstadt-Mathildenhöhe, 1983.

KOLO MOSER
1868–1918

Koloman (Kolo) Moser (30 March 1868–18 October 1918) was the son of an employee of the 'Theresianum' (Public School for Boys), IV., 15 Favoritenstrasse. As a child he had the opportunity of watching various craftsmen at work, and this made a lasting impression on him. From 1888–1892 he attended the Academy and from 1893–1895 the Arts and Crafts School (now the Academy of Applied Arts), where he taught from 1899 on. He became a co-founder of the Secession in 1897 and left it in 1905 with the Klimt group; and of the "Wiener Werkstätte", which he left in 1908. In 1905 he married an ex-pupil, Editha Mautner-Markhof, a match that solved his financial problems for good. In 1900/01 he commissioned Josef Hoffmann to build him a house at XIX., Hohe Warte (see map p. VII/7) and–much influenced by Ferdinand Hodler–began to paint. Being an incredibly gifted artist, everything he turned his hand to was first-class. He was a close friend of Josef Hoffmann's, who recorded how fruitful their collaboration was and how inspired he was by Moser's flight of fancy. His work is scattered all over the world–maybe one reason why there has so far been no catalogue raisonné.

Kolo Moser, his wife Ditha and his two children. Photograph, about 1909.

View of Moser's first studio, III., 36 Rennweg, designed by Josef Hoffmann, no longer extant. Photograph, about 1900.

Josef Hoffmann in the chair he designed in 1898 for Moser's studio, and which is typical of his early style. Photograph, about 1900.

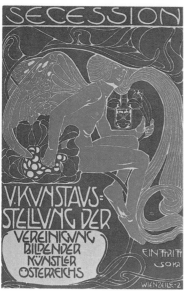

Above: Working drawing for the leading of a glass window (no longer extant) in the Secession building. (From Ver Sacrum II/1899, Library of the Academy of Fine Arts).

Hermann Bahr (1863–1934), propagator of the Secession, wrote the wording that runs round the window: "THE ARTIST SHOWS HIS OWN WORLD: THE BEAUTY THAT WAS BORN WITH HIM, THAT WAS NOT BEFORE AND WILL NEVER COME AFTER."

Left: Poster for the 5ᵗʰ Secession exhibition, 1899 (Hist. Museum).

*Poster for the 13ᵗʰ Exhibition of
the Secession (Hist. Museum).*

"Ver Sacrum" appeared from 1898 to 1903. From the visual point of view it is the finest German-language periodical of the "Jugendstil" (Art nouveau) era. Its make-up and typography influenced book printing in Austria.

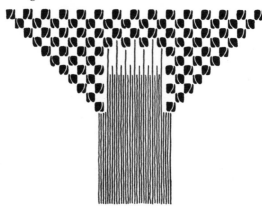

"A decorative patch in red and green . . ." Colour lithograph in "Ver Sacrum" I/1898, No 1. (Library of the Academy of Fine Arts).

Two jackets designed by Kolo Moser for "Ver Sacrum" (I/1898, No 2 and II/1899, No 4; Library of the Academy of Fine Arts).

Writing-desk with sliding seat. Formerly the property of Fritz Waerndorfer, the "Wiener Werkstätte's" first financier (Mus. f. angew. Kunst).

Buffet: "The Big Haul", 1900 (Mus. f. angew. Kunst).

Kolo Moser has up to now been far too little appreciated as the pioneer of exhibition technique that he was. Above: Secession, 18th exhibition, dedicated entirely to Klimt, 1903. Below: 10th exhibition, 1901. On the wall Klimt's "Medicine", 1901. Both catalogues in the Library of the Academy of Fine Arts (Inner City Map No 19).

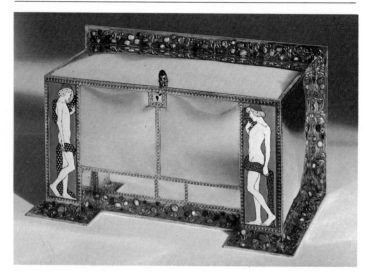

Above: Casket, Silver, with semi-precious stones (Mus. f. angew. Kunst).

Below: Jardinière and vase: perforated metal (Mus. f. angew. Kunst).

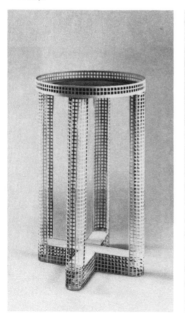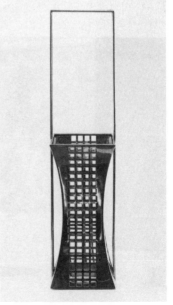

Moser designed the finest postage stamps for the Austro-Hungarian monarchy. Except for the landscape series those shown belong to the set published on the occasion of Emperor Francis Joseph's Jubilee, 1908. First row: Imperial Castle, Vienna; Schönbrunn Castle, Vienna. Second row: Emperor Karl VI; Empress Maria Theresia; Emperor Joseph II. Third row: views from Bosnia-Herzegowina. Fourth row: Emperor Francis Joseph I and insignia.

WHERE TO FIND:

APPLIED ARTS, FURNITURE, DESIGNS:
Mus. f. angew. Kunst = Museum für angewandte Kunst (Museum of Applied Arts), I., Stubenring (Inner City Map No 4). The Library houses the "Wiener Werkstätte Archives" (at present difficult to consult). Open: Tues., Wed., Fri. 10−16 hours, Thurs. 10−18 hours, Sun. 10−13 hours. Closed on Mondays and Saturdays.

"VER SACRUM" AND CATALOGUES OF THE SECESSION:
Akademie der bildenden Künste, I., 1 Schillerplatz (Inner City Map No 19). Library open: Tues., Thurs., Fri. 10−14 hours, Wed. 10−13, 15−18 hours, Sat. 9−13 hours. Closed on Mondays.

DESIGNS FOR POSTAGE STAMPS:
Archives of "Generaldirektion für die Post- und Telegraphenverwaltung", I., 8 Postgasse. (At present not open to the public; there are plans, however, for future exhibitions.)

POSTERS:
Hist. Mus. = Historisches Museum der Stadt Wien (City of Vienna Historical Museum), IV., Karlsplatz (Inner City Map No 15). Open: Tues., Wed., Fri. 10−16 hours, Thurs. 10−19 hours, Sat. 14−18 hours, Sun. 9−17 hours. Closed on Mondays.

GRAVE:
Koloman Moser's grave is at "Hietzinger Friedhof" (Hietzing cemetery), Underground station "Hietzing"; from there, a 10 minutes' walk to Maxingstrasse and cemetery entrance), group 16, grave No 14.

Literature:
Fenz, Werner: Kolo Moser. Internationaler Jugendstil und Wiener Secession. Salzburg 1976.
Koloman Moser, 1868−1918. Catalogue of the Museum of Applied Arts, Vienna 1979.
Koloman Moser. Herausgegeben von der österreichischen Post- und Telegraphenverwaltung (chiefly designs for postage stamps), Vienna, 1964.
Nebehay, Christian M., Ver Sacrum 1898−1903. Vienna 1982. There is also an English edition, London & New York 1982.

JOSEF HOFFMANN
1870–1956

JOSEF HOFFMANN · 1870–1956

Josef Hoffmann was born on December 15th, 1870, as the only son of a well-to-do cotton manufacturer who was a house-owner and mayor of Pirnitz near Iglau in Moravia. (Below: a view of Pirnitz drawn by Hoffmann and featured in the Secession's 5th catalogue.) In 1889, after secondary school, he entered, together with Adolf Loos, the Technical College at Brünn (Brno, Czechoslovakia). In 1891 he worked at the Military Office of Works at Würzburg, Germany. From 1892 on he studied at the Vienna Academy under Carl v. Hasenauer (1833–1894) and Otto Wagner (1841–1918) and was one of the latter's best pupils. In 1895 he won the Rome Prize and set up on his own. He was a founding member of the Secession in 1897 and a lifelong friend of Klimt's. In 1903 he founded, together with Kolo Moser and the financier Fritz Waerndorfer, the "Wiener Werkstätte". He was an excellent architect, an outstanding interior decorator and a brilliant craftsman. The catalogue of his buildings and projects runs to 502 items; but there is as yet no *catalogue raisonné* of his output in the applied arts. Although now internationally famous, he was almost forgotten in his last years. He had an astonishing genius for improvisation; unshakable imperturbability; and a gift for friendship, especially towards the young, among them Oskar Kokoschka and Egon Schiele, both of whom worked for a short time at the "Wiener Werkstätte". When the "WW" folded up in 1932, little more was heard of this once so honoured man, who all his life had been quiet and modest of bearing. Oddly enough, although he came of a well-to-do family, Hoffmann never built himself a house of his own. He married twice; his son Wolfgang emigrated to the United States in 1925. Hoffmann died on May 7th, 1956 and is buried in the "Wiener Zentralfriedhof" (Central Cemetery, XI., Vienna, Group 14 C).

Josef Hoffmann created an office for the Secession (above) and the so-called "Ver Sacrum Room" (below). "Ver Sacrum" (Sacred Spring) was the title of the periodical issued by the Secession between 1898 and 1903 with the intention of propagating its ideas. The years between 1898 and 1905, before the Klimt group left the Secession, came to be known as the "Viennese Art Spring".

Hoffmann's "Ver Sacrum" room, typical of his early style, but unfortunately no longer extant, gave rise to a serious controversy, since Adolf Loos had hoped to get the contract. It culminated, in 1908, in Loos' famous polemic on "Ornament and Crime"—an unveiled criticism of the 1908 "Kunstschau" (Art Show).

A corner of a living-room (Ver Sacrum, III/1900, p. 69) (Albertina).

Hoffmann drew a great number of illustrations for the first issues of "Ver Sacrum". They are partly ornamental margins, vignettes and borders, and partly (see above) projects for interior decoration, furnishings and—among others—for an exhibition pavilion (below, possibly for the Secession building). All these illustrations are important examples of his early style.

From the very first Hoffmann drew his clients from the ranks of the upper middle class, who were receptive to all things modern. In 1900 one of the most interesting personalities in the monarchy, Karl Wittgenstein, industrialist and patron of the Viennese Secessionists, commissioned Hoffmann to build him a forester's house at No 105 Hohenberg in Lower Austria (below); and among other commissions Hoffmann also built him, in 1906, a hunting lodge at Hochreith in Lower Austria (still extant). Another member of the Wittgenstein family, Paul, had Hoffmann adapt and furnish his country house "Bergerhöhe" near Hohenberg (above) in 1899 and his apartment in Vienna in 1916/17.

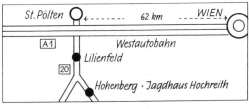

Villa of Dr. Hugo Henneberg at XIX., 8 Wollergasse (contemporary photograph). The house, which was characteristic of Hoffmann's early work, was completely altered after 1946.

The semi-detached houses of Kolo Moser, XIX., 6 Steinfeldgasse, and Carl Moll, XIX., 8 Steinfeldgasse (seen below in a photograph taken from the garden in 1966) have been altered. Moll's house in particular is barely recognizable today.

Of the four residential houses built by Hoffmann on the Hohe Warte (a fifth, the Villa Ast, XIX., 2 Steinfeldgasse / 12 Wollergasse, was commissioned in 1909 and completed in 1911), the last one, built in 1902 for Dr. Friedrich Spitzer at XIX., 4 Steinfeldgasse (above) is the best preserved.

1 *Villa Henneberg, 1901*
2 *Villa Ast, 1911 (see also page VII/16)*
3 *Villa Spitzer, 1902*
4 *Villa Moser-Moll I, 1901*

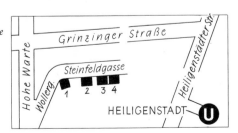

At the Secession's 14th exhibition, Max Klinger's "Beethoven" statue was given a reception no other work of art of the time had known. The artists who decorated the rooms gave their services free of charge, among them Klimt who painted his "Beethoven Frieze" for the lefthand room. Hoffmann was responsible for the arrangement of the exhibits.

Hoffmann created a "supraporte" consisting of chiselled mortar in a remarkably abstract geometrical pattern (no longer extant). All the decorative panels by Kolo Moser, Maximilian Lenz and Emil Orlik were, indeed, spectacularly modern.

Above: Showroom of the Wiener Werkstätte at VII., 32 Neustiftgasse (no longer extant; photograph, 1904).

In its 30 years' existence the "Wiener Werkstätte", founded on May 19th, 1903, produced work of exemplary beauty in all branches of arts and crafts. Josef Hoffmann and Kolo Moser (until 1908) were its artistic directors. Vienna was full of accomplished craftsmen. There was, however, a dearth of modern designers —and this is where Hoffmann's main achievement lay. He had a way of getting gifted young craftsmen to work with him, and was tireless in his search for new talent.

Charles R. Mackintosh (1868—1928) strongly influenced the "Wiener Werkstätte" in its beginnings. He had come to Vienna in 1900 to visit the Secession's great arts and crafts exhibition, and had also worked in Fritz Waerndorfer's house. Waerndorfer was the first to finance the "Wiener Werkstätte"; he was followed, in 1913, by the Primavesi family and, from 1926 on, by Kuno Grohmann. In spite of its artistic success the enterprise had to be closed down in 1932 for lack of a solid commercial basis.

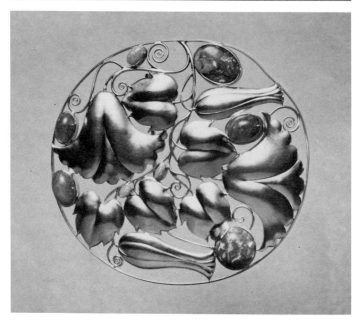

Hoffmann's creative imagination encompassed all the various branches of craftsmanship. His work covered furniture, silver, glass, porcelain and leather; and he even tried his hand at a new form of the artistic postcard. The objects shown here are chosen from those on exhibition at the "Museum für angewandte Kunst" (Inner City Map No 4). Above: Brooch, about 1905. Below left: Samovar, silver, 1904; right: Cutlery for Fritz Waerndorfer, silver, 1904. All this is from Hoffmann's early years, later the plain lines were abandoned in favour of a certain baroque opulence.

Apart from arranging exhibition rooms, Hoffmann was a genius for improvising pavilions. He had an unrivalled gift for designing makeshift buildings that looked as if they were made to last for eternity. The most important among them were the pavilions for the "Kunstschau" in Vienna (1908), the International Art Exhibition in Rome in 1911 (above), the Werkbund (Arts and Crafts Society) Exhibition in Cologne in 1914, and his design for the Secession pavilion at the World Fair in St. Louis in 1904 (below)— a project that never materialized.

One of Hoffmann's most important buildings is the former "Sanatorium Westend" (1904), commonly known as the "Purkersdorf Sanatorium", built for Professor Victor Zuckerkandl and originally destined to house mental patients. The building stands in a large park at No 74 Wiener Strasse, a road leading westwards out of the city. Today it is only a shadow of its former self: Leopold Bauer added another floor in 1926—against Hoffmann's will—and thus robbed it of its character. Only a few pieces of the original furniture have remained.

Below: Main dining-hall (not preserved).

One of the chairs designed for the Sanatorium at Purkersdorf (Mus. f. angew. Kunst, Inner City Map No 47).
Compare illustration on opposite page, below, where this admirably functional piece of furniture is clearly discernible.

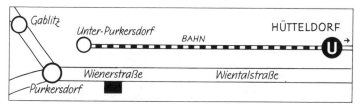

Hoffmann's masterpiece is to be found, not in Vienna but in Brussels at 281 Avenue Tervueren. Built in 1905–11, the "palais" is still in in the hands of the Stoclet family. It is, however, almost impossible to get permission to view the interior, which has been excellently preserved. The materials used both outside and inside were of the best quality obtainable; and the interior, conceived as a whole, is of timeless beauty down to the smallest detail.

Above: General view; below: Main hall.

The dining-room marks a culmination in interior decoration. The walls are decorated with Klimt's famous "Stoclet" frieze (inlaid marble).

One of Hoffmann's buildings that has come down to us with only slight alterations to its exterior is the villa he designed in 1909−1911 at XIX., 2 Steinfeldgasse / 12 Wollergasse (see also plan p. VII/7) for the well-to-do building contractor Eduard Ast. This villa, with its elegance and quality of design, may be said to be one of Hoffmann's best private houses.

Villa Skywa-Primavesi. View of the building's left wing. The sculpture is by Anton Hanak (1875–1934).

Another garden villa still in an excellent state of preservation is that built for Josefine Skywa and Robert Primavesi in 1913–1915 at XIII., 18 Gloriettegasse. It is now the property of the Trade Unions Council and has been converted into a training centre.

The home of Edmund Bernatzik (1854−1919) at XIX., 28 Spring-siedelgasse (above, view from the garden) is practically unaltered. Both this house and the virtually intact group of eight homes known as the Kaasgraben Estate at XIX., Kaasgrabengasse and Suttingergasse (below) were built in 1912−1913.

The best-preserved of Hoffmann's houses is to be found at XIX., 22 Nusswaldgasse. It was built for Sonja Knips in 1924/25 from plans dated 1919 and has been carefully looked after by the present owners. (Above: garden. Below: view from the street). Klimt's portrait of Sonja Knips is in the Österreichische Galerie.

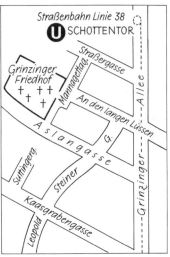

In 1911 Alma Mahler-Werfel (1879–1964) commissioned Hoffmann to design a tombstone for her first husband, composer Gustav Mahler (1860–1911). (Grinzing cemetery, group 7, row 2).

The Otto Wagner monument (below) was originally situated at a more spectacular site outside the railings of the "Volksgarten", opposite the Chancery. It now stands next to the Akademie der bildenden Künste (Academy of Fine Arts), I., Makartgasse.

Above: Salesroom of the "Wiener Werkstätte" fashion department, I., 41 Kärntnerstrasse, above (no longer extant).

As an interior decorator Hoffmann set the highest standards. He aimed at a total effect: colour of the walls, curtains, floor coverings and paint—everything matched down to the smallest detail; nothing was left to chance. The craftsmen he employed were the top men in their respective fields. The showroom of the "Wiener Werkstätte" (fashion department) was at the Palais Esterházy, I., 41 Kärntnerstrasse. The textiles department was situated at I., 32 Kärntnerstrasse, whereas the main salesroom was for many years at I., 15 Graben. Unfortunately nearly all of Hoffmann's shop interiors and premises in Vienna were dismantled. An exception is the entrance of the sweet shop "Altmann & Kühne" (below left), I., 30 Graben, built in 1932 together with O. Haerdtl.

From 1928—32 Hoffmann built a block of 332 flats for the Vienna Town Council at X., 94 Laxenburger Strasse. In later years the outer walls were drastically altered (removal of the plaster stripes, extension of the attics, etc.). The façades on the inner (courtyard) side still convey an idea of the architect's intentions.

In 1930—32 Hoffmann built four estate houses for the "Werkbund Siedlung" (Arts and Crafts Union Housing Estate) at XIII., 79—85 Veitingergasse, consisting of two types, both arranged symmetrically and relatively well preserved.

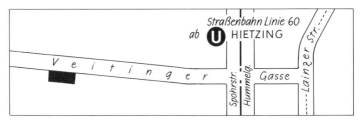

In 1820–23 Peter Nobile (1774–1854) built the "Theseus Temple" in the Volksgarten, a copy of the Theseion in Athens. The temple was destined to house a sculpture group "Theseus vanquishes the Minotaur" by Antonio Canova (1757–1854) which had been acquired by Emperor Francis I. When in 1890 the group was transferred to the main staircase of the Kunsthistorisches Museum, the "Theseus Temple" was left empty and remained so except for an occasional exhibition. In 1936, the painter Carl Moll (1861–1945), a member of the Secession and an important personality in Vienna's artistic circles, suggested the installation of a pantheon of Austria's great musicians. Hoffmann jumped at the idea and worked out a project with candelabra placed in three niches and steps leading down to a crypt which was to house the remains of twelve of Austria's greatest composers. In view of the fact that Austria possesses neither a pantheon nor any burial place for her famous sons comparable to Westminster Abbey, Hoffmann's project would have been well worth taking up.

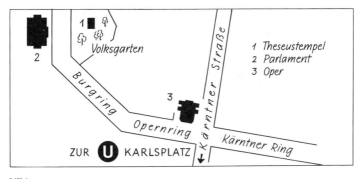

WHERE TO FIND:

BUILDINGS (see also in the text):
Sanatorium Purkersdorf, closed down since 1975: Purkersdorf, Lower Austria, 74 Wiener Strasse (see map page VII/13). Visits are possible. Phone Vienna 43 12 19.

OBJECTS D'ART, JEWELLERY, SILVER, DESIGNS:
Österreichisches Museum für angewandte Kunst (Mus. f. angew. Kunst), I., 1 Stubenring (Inner City Map No 4), Library; "Wiener Werkstätte Archives" (at present difficult to consult). Open: Tues., Wed., Fri. 10−16 hours, Thurs. 10−18 hours, Sun. 10−13 hours. Closed on Mondays and Saturdays.

Hist. Museum = Historisches Museum der Stadt Wien (City of Vienna Historical Museum), IV., Karlsplatz (Inner City Map No 15). Open: Tues., Wed., Fri. 10−16 hours, Thurs. 10−19 hours, Sat. 14−18 hours, Sun. 9−17 hours. Closed on Mondays.

GLASS:
Glass Museum of J. & L. Lobmeyr, I., 26 Kärntnerstrasse (Inner City Map No 44). Open: Mon.−Fri. 9−18 hours, Sat. 9−13 hours. Closed on Sundays (see below: a glass set designed for Lobmeyr by Josef Hoffmann).

Literature:
Gresleri, Giuliano, Josef Hoffmann, Bologna 1981.
Nebehay, Christian M., Ver Sacrum 1898−1903, Vienna 1982. English edition: London & New York 1982.
Schweiger, Werner J., Wiener Werkstätte. Kunst und Handwerk 1903−1932, Vienna 1982.
Sekler, Eduard F., Josef Hoffmann. Das architektonische Werk, Salzburg 1982.

ADOLF LOOS
1870–1933

ADOLF LOOS 1870–1933

Adolf Loos (Brünn, 10th December 1870–Kalksburg near Vienna, 23rd August 1933) was undoubtedly one of the most interesting and important of Vienna's modern architects. He was an innovator, an uncompromising fighter, and an aesthete: one who devoted his undivided attention to every single object in a room, however small (to name two instances: a coal chute under a removable doormat; and mothproof, ventilated cupboards). He made the best of even the most restricted space (Loos Bar) and thought up the most economical building methods for his houses (e. g. interior walls made of plaster). He defended his theories in stirring lectures that were almost always sold out, and did not hesitate to voice his opinions in public. The dictum *"ORNAMENT IS A CRIME"*, however, which spread his fame far beyond the architectural world, was never pronounced by him: it is, rather, the bowdlerized title of an article of his, *"ORNAMENT AND CRIME"*. His very first building, the "Loos House" on the Michaelerplatz, built in 1911/12, caused one of the major scandals of the period. Its radically modern façade was a slap in the general public's face. Nicknames for it were legion: "Silo", "Dustbin", "Prison", "Cigarette lighter", "Marble coalbin" . . . Nowadays it is regarded as a fine example of modern architecture.

Loos was of a quarrelsome nature, and so he made enemies of, or at least had differences of opinion with, many of his contemporaries. On the other hand he was capable of real friendship: he was full of loving care for his girl friend, the dancer Bessie Bruce, and paid for her stay at the clinic in Leysin where she lay for years with tuberculosis. He was also a friend of the Viennese poet Peter Altenberg: they loved to spend the night together in bars, occasionally quarrelling over a dancer for whom both had conceived a sudden passion. Another of Loos' friends was Karl Kraus, who spoke up for him in his periodical "Die Fackel". And it was he, Loos, who sponsored and supported Oskar Kokoschka during his difficult early years.

Loos struck a new note in the coffeehouse life of his time: he was what may be called the first coffeehouse architect. For years, having no studio of his own, he would sketch those brilliant projects of his between one cup of coffee and the next, often on cash vouchers borrowed from the waiters. As an architect he did his best work before the First World War; after 1918 he found it difficult to get commissions. He worked part of his time in Paris and in Czechoslovakia, whence he drew a pension from 1930 onwards. He died in poverty. A great deal of his work was destroyed. It must, however, be remembered that in those days architects imposed their will–and their visions–on their clients: there were Loos houses in which literally every piece of furniture was fitted except for one chair which was just about the only movable object in the house. Later generations, feeling hemmed-in and coerced, destroyed those clever, modern, practical and goodlooking designs. It is for us to admire his creations and seek to preserve what is left of them.

Adolf Loos senior (1831–1879) was a sculptor and stonemason in Brünn (Brno, Czechoslovakia, today). He had studied sculpture with Franz Bauer (1797–1872) in Vienna and, with the help of his well-to-do brother, set up on his own in Brünn in 1861.

Adolf Loos was born in Brünn on 10th December, 1870. As a child, being greatly attached to his father, he spent all his spare time in the big workshop, watching accomplished craftsmen work with choice materials—an experience that proved decisive for his later career. His father's untimely death was a break in the nine-year-old's life.

The mother engaged a foreman and took over the business herself. She was thrifty to the point of denying the boy virtually everything, and the more clearly she saw that her son wanted to have nothing to do either with her or with the business, the more she turned to her two daugthers. From 1881 to 1882 Adolf attended secondary school at Iglau, where he met Josef Hoffmann. An indifferent pupil, he had to repeat classes several times; in 1885 he joined the arts and crafts schools in Reichenberg, later in Brünn. After passing his final examination in 1889, he attended the Technical College in Dresden as a special student.

In 1892 Adolf Loos went to America, the immediate incentive being the 1893 world exhibition in Chicago. At first he stayed in Philadelphia with a brother of his father's, a well-to-do watchmaker. He spent the next years in New York, roughing it and earning money where he could: as a mason, a journalist, a critic for German-language newspapers, as a marquetry worker and as a draughtsman with a master-builder. The degree to which he was influenced by modern American architecture has not yet been fully investigated. In 1896 he lived for a while in London. Meanwhile his mother had had him put under trusteeship because of his alleged extravagance; the legal dispute over his father's estate ended in his being left with a small sum after paying the lawyers. In Vienna he found a job with the architect—and subsequent town-planner—Carl Mayreder (1856–1911), whose wife Rosa (1858–1938) was a sociologist, a sufragette and the author of the libretto for Hugo Wolf's opera "Corregidor".

From 1897 on Loos began to publish critical essays. In the first issues of "Ver Sacrum"—the magazine founded by the Secession in 1898—he published two articles criticizing the Ringstrasse architecture: "The Potemkin Town" and "Our Young Architects". He had hoped for a commission to help with the interior decoration of the Secession building, but it never materialized; his later deep-rooted conflict with Josef Hoffmann may well be traced back to this disappointment. He remained a lone wolf for the rest of his life.

Of the "Café Museum", I., corner of Operngasse and Friedrich-strasse, designed by Loos in 1899, only the façade remains; the interior has been altered. Conveniently located—next to the Academy of Fine Arts, the Secession and the Technical University—it soon turned into a meetingplace for the artist set (another was the former "Café Kremser", I., 10 Kärntnerring, where the Hoffmann clan met). Loos designed all the furniture: note the use of precious woods (dark mahogany) and of polished brass set into the walls and into some of the furniture—an idea he must have got from England. Below: View of the interior, seen from the entrance. Photograph, about 1899.

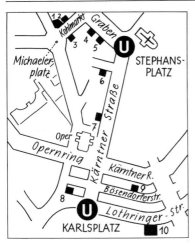

1 Loos-House on the Michaelerplatz
2 Book shop Manz
3 Cosmetics shop Ruttner
4 Gentlemen's outfitter Leschka
5 Gentlemen's outfitter Kniže
6 "American Bar"
7 Lobmeyr
8 Café Museum
9 Loos' Apartment
10 Hist. Museum

Loos and his first wife, Lina, née Obertimpfler, married on 21st July, 1902 in Eisgrub, Moravia. The bride, an actress, was 19; Peter Altenberg (1859–1919), poet and bohémien, had also been passionately in love with her. Loos settled into an apartment on the 5th floor of a house at I., 8 Giselastrasse (now Bösendorferstrasse). The living-room—slightly altered—is on show in the Historisches Museum. Below: a contemporary photograph.

Above left: The first marriage with the actress Lina Obertimpfler (1882–1950) lasted only 3 years, from 1902 to 1905.

In 1905 Loos started an affair with the 19-year-old English dancer Bessie Bruce (1886–1921). Oskar Kokoschka painted her portrait in 1909/10. She died in 1921 of tuberculosis in a clinic in Leysin, Switzerland.

From 1919 to 1926 Loos was married to the dancer Elsa (Elsie) Altmann (born 1898) who now lives in Buenos Aires (below left). Loos' third wife, whom he married in 1928, was the photographer Klara Franziska (Claire) Beck (?1905–?1945).

In 1904 Loos was commissioned by the Viennese physiologist Professor Dr. Theodor Beer (died 1919) to carry out the remodelling and interior decoration of his large property "La Maladaire" in Clarens on Lake Geneva. Loos also drew the plans for the conversion of the adjacent farm building and the connecting passage. He stopped work on the project in 1906/07. Max Fabiani was entrusted with further planning, but the actual construction was carried out by Hugo Ehrlich. Nevertheless, the Villa Karma rates as one of Loos' early works.

Above: The garden front of the Villa Karma, about 1963. Right: Loos and Professor Beer on the building site, 1904.

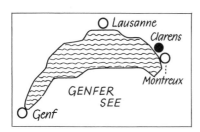

In 1908 Loos designed, in a small street in the 1ˢᵗ district connecting Kärntnerstrasse and Seilergasse, the "American Bar" (now
known as "Kärntner Bar"). The bar caused a sensation from the
moment it opened up, and although it has slightly come down in
the world, is still undoubtedly one of the showpieces of "modern"
Vienna at the turn of the century. It is incredible what Loos made
of so restricted a space (15 × 8 ft.), what effects he achieved, and
how he managed, by using the best materials available, to create
an atmosphere of timeless elegance. It is now no longer as
originally conceived by Loos, who meant it to be a stand-up bar:
the seating was put in by the proprietors.

Above: The Bar in its present state: view towards the rear wall.

Below: Front entrance in its original state, about 1930 (since altered).

THE HOUSE ON THE MICHAELERPLATZ

The house jutting into the Michaeler-square is the "Dreilauferhaus", built in 1799. The adjacent houses on the Kohlmarkt were built later in the "Ringstrasse" style. To the left the Palais Herberstein. Photograph, about 1900.

The following situation prevailed on the Michaelerplatz around 1900: the "Michaeler" (north) wing of the "Hofburg" had been completed in 1893. On the other hand, the fine baroque houses that had been the distinguishing mark of the Inner City until about 1870 had fallen victims to the building and speculation fever of the late 19th century. The Palais Herberstein, for instance, was built in the "Ringstrasse" style at the junction of Schauflergasse and Michaelerplatz, on the site of the former Dietrichstein house with its famous "literary" Café Griensteidl, the destruction of which in 1897 caused Karl Kraus to write his satirical essay "The demolition of literature". In order to clear more space for traffic in the Michaelerplatz, the "Dreilauferhaus", built in 1799 and until then jutting out into the square, was demolished and the site severely reduced in area. This plot was acquired by the outfitters Goldman & Salatsch, for whom Loos had already built premises on the Graben (no longer extant). The firm invited entries for a competition but accepted none of the eight plans submitted. Loos, who had not taken part in the competition, got the commission in 1909—his first house.

The salient feature of Loos's plan is that the house faces the centre of the square. Whether its four marble columns can really be considered to be the counterparts of those adorning St. Michael's Church on the opposite side, remains open to argument. Loos gave the ground floor and entresol an elegant marble façade (he

travelled specially to Euboea, Greece, where an ancient quarry, unused for over 2000 years, had been re-opened in Karystos), thereby creating a sharp contrast to the completely unadorned upper stories.

Situated in direct proximity to two pompous buildings in the Ringstrasse style (16 Kohlmarkt next door, and the afore-mentioned Palais Herberstein)—an unhappy constellation if ever there was one—the naked façade of the Loos house must indeed have had a provocative effect.

The façade set off a storm of protest hardly less violent than that let loose on Klimt and his University paintings. One of Loos' chief opponents was Rykl, a sculptor and manufacturer of imitation stone, who was also a member of the City Council and there coined the phrase of "this horror of a house". Work on the building had to be suspended; but the authorities authorized its continuation on 4th August, 1912, with the proviso (entered in the property register) that the bronze flower-boxes that were to be put in should be filled with greenery all the year round.

In a lecture held at the "Sofiensäle" on 11ᵗʰ December 1911 before an audience of 2000, Loos defended "his" house.

The staircase laid out in flecked Skyros marble has remained practically unaltered.

The interior—which, apart from some elements transferred to the Ruttner cosmetics shop at I., 11 Kohlmarkt, is no longer extant —was as up to date as the firm itself. In addition to departments for hunting, riding, polo, tennis and automobile outfits, there was, as early as in 1911, a winter sports department with skis on sale. Moreover, the house boasted a "private training school" for employees with classrooms and workshops—not to mention the excellently equipped ateliers (cutting-shops, ironing room, shirt room, etc.). The firm went bankrupt in 1925/26.

Salesroom of the Sports Department, ground floor. Note the glass showcases around the dark pillars (photograph appr. 1912).

Between 1897 and 1919 Loos carried out various commissions. Of these, only twelve have survived more or less unaltered, among them the premises of the tailoring firm Kniže, I., 13 Graben: here, exceptionally, both portal and interior have remained unchanged. It is not known whether Loos also built the Kniže branch in Karlsbad; he was, however, entrusted with those in Berlin and Paris (Champs Elysées).

It was no accident that Loos was *the* architect of the Viennese outfitters (his first commission was in 1897, for the court tailor Ebenstein, I., 5 Kohlmarkt—no longer extant). Loos himself was given to extravagant elegance and had just a hint of the English dandy about him.

The photographs, taken in 1930, show the sales room on the ground floor (below right) and the fitting rooms in the entresol (above and below left). The interior is practically unchanged to this day.

The bookshop Manz, I., 16 Kohlmarkt, was designed by Loos in 1912. The portal is practically unchanged, whereas the interior decoration was replaced.

Below: in spite of some alterations, the façade and main hall of this branch of the Zentralsparkasse at VII., 70 Mariahilfer Strasse still convey the original impression of Loos' design for the former Anglo-Austrian Bank.

The premises of the outfitter Leschka at I., 16 Graben (formerly I., 13 Spiegelgasse) were designed by Loos in 1923 and are still for the most part unchanged.

The house of Hugo and Lilly Steiner, XIII., 10 St. Veit-Gasse, was built in 1910 and is Loos's best-known villa. The photographs, taken around 1930, show (left) the view from the road and (right) from the garden.

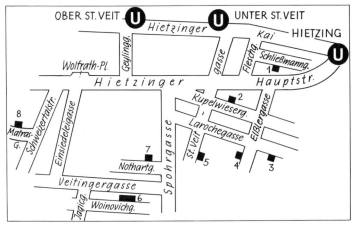

Right: The house of Dr. Otto and Auguste Stoessl, XIII., 20 Matrasgasse, 1911/12. An inexpensive home with an additional attic floor, making four floors in all.

Key to the above plan:
1 *Villa Rufer*
2 *Strasser*
3 *Scheu*
4 *Reitler*
5 *Steiner*
6 *Werkbund Siedlung ("Arts and Crafts Union" housing estate)*
7 *Horner*
8 *Stoessl*

The house of Helene Horner, XIII., 7 Nothardgasse, 1912. An equally inexpensive house. With the half-barrel-vaulting of its copper plated roof it closely resembles the Steiner villa (see opposite page).

The house of Dr. Gustav and Helene Scheu, XIII., 3 Larochegasse, 1912/13. A terrace house. The top floor has its own separate street entrance. The building authorities originally insisted on the façade being overgrown. This was the first terrace house in Central Europe.

The villa of Hilde and Karl Strasser, XIII., 28 Kupelwiesergasse, 1918/19. This house, originally built in 1896, was converted by Loos. The interior fittings are still extant (green onyx panelling in the dining-room, library).

The house of Josef and Maria Rufer, XIII., 11 Schliessmanngasse, 1922. To quote Heinrich Kulka, Loos's trusty assistant: ". . . The standard type for a house of this size. It cannot be improved upon."

The country house of Paul Khuner at Kreuzberg near Payerbach, Lower Austria, 1929/30. Loos's sketches were carried out by his assistant Heinrich Kulka (1900–1974). The house was constructed with block elements and had a large, high entrance hall surrounded by a gallery.

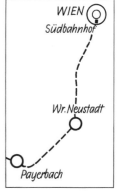

The purpose of the "Werkbund" (Arts and Crafts Union) housing estate in XIII., 13, 15, 17 and 19 Woinovichgasse (1930) was to foster inexpensive homes. The best architects of the post-war period took part: there were houses by Loos (with Kulka), Lurçat, Neutra, Plischke, Hoffmann, Holzmeister and Haerdtl. The semi-detached Loos−Kulka houses (above) cover an area of 18 × 13 ft. each.

Apart from his furniture designs, Loos did not dabble in applied arts. Only relatively late, in 1931, did he design glass for the well-known Vienna firm of Lobmeyr. Although he himself was not entirely satisfied with the end-product, the service he designed became very popular and is still being manufactured. (Glass Museum, Lobmeyr; I., 26 Kärntnerstrasse; see map p. VIII/7).

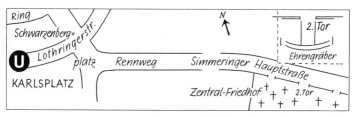

Tombstone for Peter Altenberg at the Vienna Central Cemetery, 2nd gate (Group O, Row 1, No 84), 1919. Inscription: "He loved and saw it all".

Inscription by the poet Altenberg on a photograph (right): "Architect Loos and Peter Altenberg! Two men who disregarded all the mistakes of the past!", 1918.

Adolf Loos' grave at the Vienna Central Cemetery, 2nd gate, section 32 c of the Graves of Honour. It was constructed by his pupil and assistant Heinrich Kulka from sketches which Loos had drawn during the last year of his life. The costs were met by his friends.

WHERE TO FIND:

BUILDINGS see text.

DOCUMENTS, PLANS, SKETCHES, PHOTOGRAPHS:
Graphische Sammlung Albertina (Albertina), I., 1 Augustinerstrasse (Inner City Map No 24), Printroom (also the Loos Archives). Open: Mon., Tues., Wed., Thurs. 13−16 hours, closed Fri.−Sun.

GLASS:
"Glasmuseum" of J. & L. Lobmeyr, I., 26 Kärntnerstrasse (Inner City Map No 44). Open: Tues., Wed., Fri. 10−16 hours, Thurs. 10−18 hours, Sun. 10−13 hours; closed Mo. & Sat.

LIVING ROOM (formerly at I., 8 Bösendorferstrasse), today Historisches Museum der Stadt Wien (Hist. Museum), IV., Karlsplatz (Inner City Map No 15). Open: Tues., Wed., Fri. 10−16 hours, Thurs. 10−19 hours, Sat. 14−18 hours, Sun. 9−17 hours. Closed on Monday.

Literature:
Altmann-Loos, Elsie: Adolf Loos, der Mensch, Vienna 1968.
Czech, Hermann; Mistelbauer, Wolfgang: Das Loos-Haus, Vienna 1977[2].
Loos, Adolf: Die Potemkinsche Stadt (and other essays). Reprint. Vienna 1963.
Loos, Adolf: Ins Leere gesprochen. Essays 1897−1900. Reprint. Vienna 1982.
Loos, Adolf: Trotzdem. Essays 1900−1930. Reprint. Vienna 1982.
Rukschcio, Burkhard; Schachel, Roland: Adolf Loos. Leben und Werk. Salzburg 1982.